ACTING ON PRINCIPLE

AN ESSAY ON KANTIAN ETHICS

ACTING ON PRINCIPLE

AN ESSAY ON KANTIAN ETHICS

Onora Nell

Columbia University Press
New York

The Andrew W. Mellon Foundation, through a special grant, has assisted the Press in publishing this volume.

Library of Congress Cataloging in Publication Data

Nell, Onora.
　　Acting on principle: an essay on Kantian ethics.

　　Bibliography: p.
　　Includes index.
　　1. Kant, Immanuel, 1724–1804—Ethics.　I. Title.
B2799.E8N43　　　　170　　　　74-20647
ISBN 0-231-03848-8

For

R. M. G.

PREFACE

I first came to think about acting on principle on the rebound from a brief and strong enthusiasm for utilitarianism. I was impressed with the scope, fertility, and precision of that ethical theory; then distressed by its strong and implausible premises. The very precision which had beguiled me now seemed spurious and hence dangerous. But I remained sure that a moral theory which was not fruitful, which could not guide action, was pointless. Without much hope I began looking at some Kantian ethical theories, such as those of Baier and Hare, and parts of Singer. These theories construe the supreme principle of morality as enjoining a test of principles by appeal to one or another concept of universality. Some of these theories met my demand for plausibility, but none seemed able to guide action. Even though they might show which principles were moral principles, they did not show how to determine which acts a person ought or might do. Most of these theories lacked any account of the connection between principles and acts. They could not determine which of the many principles that apply to a given act it was relevant to assess; and without a solution to the problem of relevance universality tests of principles are impotent.

I had little hope that Kant's own ethical theory would satisfy my demands any better than recent and, as I supposed, clearer theories. Kant's commentators and imitators, while sharing his enthusiasm for the lofty austerity of the Categorical Imperative, have mainly regarded it as a failure. Some have thought it too meager a principle to guide action; others that it led straight to rigorism—to a senseless uniformity of action which disregards the subtle diversity of human circumstances. As I worked on Kant's writings, I came to believe that neither of these charges can be made to stick. The Categorical Imperative can guide action and does not lead to rigorism.

A main purpose of this book is to show that Kant has a solution to the problem of relevance; that the Categorical Imperative can therefore guide action, and does so with considerable precision.

However, this work is not only an interpretation of Kant. I have treated the Kantian texts with respect, and have paid erratic attention to the huge secondary literature, but my interest is less in exegesis than in argument. It is only because I believe I have found in Kant's ethics a theory which is fruitful and detailed and useful that I think I have a good reason for writing a book on ethics.

Since my book concentrates on the application of Kantian ethical theory, I shall spend little time on Kant's theory of human freedom and action or the vexing problem of reconciling his epistemology with his ethics. Nor shall I take up the problem of how the Categorical Imperative is to be justified or grounded. I do not doubt the importance of justification, but I believe a principle which cannot help us act is not worth "justifying." The first requirement for a refurbished Kantian ethics is to show that the Categorical Imperative can help us solve some of the moral problems we all confront.

The agenda is as follows: chapters 1 and 2 set out some of the criteria which any satisfactory account of acting on principle must meet. I discuss the logical structure of practical principles in chapter 1, and in chapter 2 show why an ethical theory which demands action on principle cannot be action-guiding without a theory of relevance. Chapters 3, 4, and 5 turn to Kant's ethics and are the most nearly exegetical in the book. Chapter 3 examines Kant's theory of relevance, chapter 4 his basic ethical categories, and chapter 5 the method by which the Categorical Imperative can be used to assign acts to these categories. Chapter 6 steps back from the Kantian texts to consider what his theory achieves and concludes that Kant has an impressive theory of moral worth but a vulnerable theory of right. Chapter 7 is devoted to a consideration of the extent of this vulnerability and of some ways in which it could be remedied. The writing of this book has been a rather solitary enterprise. Hence the few debts of gratitude I owe are perhaps deeper than usual. It is a pleasure to thank Russell Grice, Edward Nell, Robert Nozick, John Rawls, and Robert Schultz.

Barnard College   Onora Nell
New York City
September 1974

CONTENTS

ACTING ON PRINCIPLE

AN ESSAY ON KANTIAN ETHICS

CHAPTER ONE

PRINCIPLES OF ACTION

I Formality and Fertility

It is commonly believed that if we are to do what is right and good we need to have moral principles and to act on these principles, or at least not against them. Philosophical writings on ethics include a long tradition of analyzing how principles should be selected and how acts can be aligned with principles. The most famous analysis is Kant's discussion of the Categorical Imperative, the "supreme principle of morality," as a test of the universality of the principles on which agents act, which he intended to reveal both whether they acted on principle and the moral status of their acts. He formulated the Categorical Imperative in a number of ways, of which the best known demands that we

Act only on that maxim through which you can at the same time will that it should become a universal law.[1]

The appeal of this principle to Kant was its combination of formality and fertility. He thought that its presuppositions were meager, perhaps wholly formal, and yet that it was powerful in guiding us to do morally acceptable acts.

There are numerous latterday descendants of this famous ancestor, which sometimes have only a rather remote family resemblance to it or indeed to one another. But their proponents share Kant's hope that they have produced a necessary condition on moral actions which, if not strictly speaking formal, is still parsimonious in its presuppositions, and yet useful in guiding action.

I can see no reason why large consequences should not sometimes flow from meager premises, but the conjunction is generally suspect. Most commentators on Kant's ethics have thought that he fails to show that the Categorical Imperative can guide action, and most revisions of that principle are

[1] *G.* p. 421. For an explanation of Kant citations see Bibliography.

not thought, even by their proponents, to be as powerful guides to action as Kant thought the Categorical Imperative to be. I believe, on the contrary, that the Categorical Imperative can help us make moral choices and so is worth pursuing.

I shall not here raise many questions about the justification of the Categorical Imperative. To some this will seem misguided. Why take the time to work out the implications of a principle whose justification is not established? My own view is that we can understand the Categorical Imperative clearly only after looking at its implications. I shall therefore examine its fertility in detail, but shall not argue here for its formality. Still I believe that it is in a reasonably clear sense a formal principle that might be rationally justified. My procedure arises from a strong conviction that it is a waste of time and effort to pursue the justification of principles which are not known to be helpful in guiding moral choice. I have no global criticism of metaethics to make, but consider its pursuit warranted only if it makes a difference in what we do.

The sorts of questions which I shall be asking of various universality tests on principles therefore concern their fertility or capacity to guide action:

Does a particular universality test provide a decision procedure for picking out morally acceptable principles? Or, if not for morally acceptable principles in general, then perhaps for some subset of these such as acceptable principles of right? Does a particular universality test state a necessary condition either on morally acceptable principles or on some subset of them? What exactly is the procedure for applying the universality test to principles of action? Does it provide a decision procedure (or a necessary condition) for the moral acceptability (or some types of moral acceptability) of acts? Is the proposed universality test equally useful when we assess our own or others' acts?

II Moral Principles and Morally Acceptable Principles

If the Categorical Imperative and other universality tests guide action by picking out some principles from others, then we need to see which class (or classes) of principles are picked out. Is it simply the class of moral principles which is to be selected? And here, right at the outset, we meet an ambiguity in the sense of the term "moral." For "moral" may be taken in at least two senses. There is a broad sense in which *moral* contrasts with *nonmoral,* and a narrower in which it contrasts with *immoral.* When we speak of moral questions, disputes, reasons, arguments, issues, and so on, it is the broader sense which we have in mind. When we speak of moral acts or persons, it is the narrower sense which we use. When we speak of moral principles, rules, maxims, and judgments the ambiguity is less easy to resolve. Singer, for instance, writes: ". . . a moral rule, as I shall understand the term, is simply a proposition to the effect that a certain kind of action is generally right or generally wrong." [2]

Leaving aside the implied restriction of moral rules to rules governing the rightness or wrongness of acts, the passage shows that he intends "moral" in the broader of the two senses mentioned. By this definition both the rule "It is right for witnesses to speak honestly" and the rule "It is not right for witnesses to speak honestly" are moral rules. Yet five lines later Singer states that "an act which violates a moral rule, or appears to do so, requires a justification," and seems to use "moral" in the narrower sense.

To avoid these ambiguities the following conventions will be adopted. The term "moral" will be used only in its broader sense, contrasting with "nonmoral." Hence there are moral issues, disputes, reasons, and so on. There are also moral principles, rules, and judgments. But only a proper subset of moral principles, rules, judgments, and so on consists of *morally acceptable* or *morally sound* principles, rules, and judgments; the principles, rules, and judgments forming the complementary of this subset are *morally unacceptable* or *morally unsound.* When speaking of acts and persons, the term "moral" will not be used.

Acts will be spoken of as *morally acceptable* or *morally unacceptable.* These terms of assessment are still at a very general level, and many works concentrate entirely on morally acceptable acts of one or another particular sort, such as right acts or obligatory acts. Persons will be spoken of as *morally worthy, morally indifferent,* or *morally unworthy.* Again these terms are very general, and different interpretations of moral worth may look, say, to the good intentions of moral agents or to their right actions. The lack of a generic term covering all these classes of acts and persons poses no problems. For all acts and persons are open to moral assessment, though they need not be so assessed; an act whose principle is nonmoral is not nonmoral but mor-

[2] M. G. Singer, *Generalization in Ethics,* p. 98.

ally acceptable in a particular way, which may be characterized as *morally indifferent*. There are no nonmoral acts or nonmoral persons as there are nonmoral principles, rules, and judgments, and nonmoral questions, arguments, and disputes.

A peculiarity of contemporary moral philosophy is that great effort has been put into delimiting the moral, in the broader sense just explicated. Since our concern in acting is not to do acts which have some moral status or other, but specifically to do morally acceptable acts, I believe this focus is mistaken. The problem is not to avoid acts which are esthetic or culinary or legal (such acts may often be morally acceptable), but to avoid morally unacceptable acts. Our concern is not to engage in moral reasoning, but to do what is morally acceptable. Substance is of more interest and importance than procedure. This is not to deny that it may turn out that one part of the substance of acting in a morally acceptable way is that we reason morally, or could so have reasoned while doing the same act.

〰 III *The Structure of Practical Principles*

Universality tests purport to discriminate at least some classes of morally acceptable principles. As a preliminary to critical examination of these tests, we must consider the structure of practical principles. Any practical principle, morally acceptable, unacceptable, or nonmoral, can be expressed by a linguistic structure consisting of a quantifier, an *agent description,* a verb, and an *act description,* in that order. Practical principles may be rendered schematically by

(1) All (none, some) who . . . . verb — — — —[3]

---

[3] The following methods of numbering will be used. Schematic practical principles and schematic instantiations of principles will be numbered with arabic numerals and prime marks enclosed in parentheses: (1), (2′), (7), etc. Occasionally a roman capital letter may be used in distinguishing schematic principles of a particular sort: (R6), (R3′), etc. This numbering will be consecutive and can be used for reference throughout the book. Sample principles, if they need labeling, will be numbered with arabic numerals and small roman letters without parentheses: 1, 1a, 2, etc. This numbering will be consecutive and can be used for reference only within each chapter section. All other definitions, meta-principles, etc. will be labeled by capital roman letters without parentheses: A, B, etc. Again, this labeling will be consecutive and can be used for reference only within chapter sections.

The blanks "· · · ·" and "– – – –" are filled by agent and act descriptions, respectively.

The quantifier of a practical principle indicates the scope of the agent description. For any agent description, F, principles may be stated for all x (any x, each x) such that Fx, for no x such that Fx, or for some x such that Fx.

The agent description of a practical principle specifies some of the features which characterize the agents to whom the principle applies. In the limiting case the agent description of a principle may be vacuous, so that the principle applies to all agents whatsoever. Usually when this is the case there are implicit restrictions on our understanding of the scope of the quantifier of the principle. Principles such as "Anyone ought to tell the truth" are understood as holding only for humans or only for speech users.

The third element of any linguistic expression of a practical principle consists of a (compound) verb. In moral principles verbs such as the following occur: "is obliged to (do)," "is permitted to omit (refrain from)," or "is praiseworthy for doing," "ought to do," "may ómit," "is allowed to," "deserves to receive," "has the right to do," "is culpable for doing." But most of these verbs can also occur in nonmoral practical principles. I shall propose no syntactic criterion delimiting the class of moral principles or any of its subsets.

The fourth and final element in a linguistic expression of a principle of form (1) specifies some features of the act which the principle enjoins on or permits, or blames or praises the agent for doing or omitting, or the treatment which the agent deserves or ought to receive.

With this preliminary account of the structure of the linguistic expression of a principle it is possible to indicate, using principles of right as an example, the variety of possible moral principles using a given act and agent description.

Let F be some agent description and let G be some act description; let Oyx be read as "x is an obligatory act for y" and $O'yx$ as "x is an obligatory omission for y." Then we may write down the following nonequivalent principles of right, (R1)–(R8). Each is here stated in terms of the notion of obligation, but they could as easily be stated in terms of permission.

It can be seen from an inspection of this list that there might in fact be 16 syntactically distinct principles of right if each of (R1)–(R8) was formulated both for some G act and for any G act. However, we cannot be obliged to do

(R1) (x) $(Fx \supset (\exists y)$ $(Gy$ & $Oyx))$ / All F's are obliged to do some G act.

(R2) (x) $(Fx \supset (y)$ $(Gy \supset -Oyx))$ / No F's are obliged to do any G act.

(R3) $(\exists x)$ $(Fx$ & $(\exists y)$ $(Gy$ & $Oyx))$ / Some F's are obliged to do some G act.

(R4) $(\exists x)$ $(Fx$ & (y) $(Gy \supset -Oyx))$ / Some F's are not obliged to do any G act.

(R5) (x) $(Fx \supset (y)$ $(Gy \supset O'yx))$ / All F's are obliged to refrain from any G act.

(R6) (x) $(Fx \supset (y)$ $(Gy \supset -O'yx))$ / No F's are obliged to refrain from any G act.

(R7) $(\exists x)$ $(Fx$ & (y) $(Gy \supset O'yx))$ / Some F's are obliged to refrain from any G act.

(R8) $(\exists x)$ $(Fx$ & (y) $(Gy \supset -O'yx))$ / Some F's are not obliged to refrain from any G act.

all G acts, since an indefinite number of G acts will be available whenever one is, and many of them will always be mutually exclusive. (If a debt can be discharged with cash or a check, it is not the case that the debtor is obliged both to discharge it with cash and to discharge it with a check; he is not obliged to do all possible acts which fall under the description "discharging my debts.") Hence, there are no significant principles obliging either all or some F's to do all G acts.

On the other hand, when we are not obliged to do a G act or are obliged to refrain from one, then it is not just an individual act, but a class of acts which is nonobligatory or forbidden (else such principles would be, respectively, trivially permissive and trivially prohibitive). There are no nontrivial principles stating that some or all F's are not obliged to do, or are obliged to refrain from, individual acts. (R1)–(R8) are the only significant and nontrivial principles of right.

No two of (R1)–(R8) are equivalent, though some of them follow from others. (R1) entails (R3), (R6), and (R8), while both (R2) and (R7) entail (R4). The only cases in which there would be fewer than eight possible distinct principles of right arise when the act and agent descriptions of a principle are not independent. For instance, if (R5) is interpreted as "All who are obliged to gamble are obliged to refrain from any acts of gambling" we do not need to test the resulting principle for its moral acceptability: it is not a possible practical principle. More important and less obvious cases of this sort occur when interpretations of F and G, though logically connected, are not syntactically similar. For instance, we might dismiss as impossible principles such as "All doctors are obliged to refrain from healing" or "No judges are obliged to do any sentencing." But in most contexts of decisions of right we have to choose between eight distinct possible principles of right.

Moral judgments of other sorts involve similar sorts of selection problems. For any given act and agent descriptions and a pair of two-place moral predicates, we may formulate a set of eight nonequivalent moral principles. Using "is morally worthy for doing"/"is morally worthy for refraining from" we can formulate eight nonequivalent principles of moral worth; using "deserves to receive"/"deserves not to receive" we can formulate eight nonequivalent principles of desert.

The point of a universality test on principles of action can now be seen more clearly. It should select from a set of eight possible principles of a certain type, which use a given agent and act description and a given pair of moral verbs, a subset of principles which are morally acceptable or morally sound in a particular way. It should select acceptable principles of right, acceptable principles of moral worth, or acceptable principles of desert. A universality test which performs this task may select a single principle; but even a test which does not do this may be of some use in guiding action if it shows that at least some of any set of eight practical principles are either morally acceptable or morally unacceptable. But a test which merely shows that one or more of a given set of eight principles is morally acceptable, without giving any indication as to which it is, cannot be of any use in helping moral choice. In moral choices it is not sufficient to know which principles are moral. The aim is to avoid morally unacceptable principles, not merely nonmoral principles.

I do not propose as a criterion for a universality test's being action-guiding that it be able to *generate* a set of principles on which a person in a given situation should act. Rather it should provide a method by which a person can assess any principle on which they propose to act. Wolff observes of Kant's universality test

There is no legitimate way to deduce from the Categorical Imperative those maxims which are to be ruled in as objectively binding substantive moral principles. . . .

Insofar as we undertake to act, we are bound by its strictures, just as we are bound by the strictures of the law of contradiction insofar as we undertake to judge. But the Categorical Imperative does not command any particular, substantive principle of action, any more than the law of contradiction entails any particular substantive empirical judgments.[4]

But this weakness in a universality test is more apparent than harmful. If we have a method for discriminating among proposals for action, then we can test also the proposal of inactivity. Only inaction so vegetable that the agent does not choose or propose it could not be assessed by a principle which rules on actions proposed rather than generating a set of binding moral principles for every situation. Nor is there any reason to think that a universality test will be as weak a selector of practical principles as the principle of contradiction is a weak principle for selecting among empirical judgments.

One relatively straightforward universality test on principles claims that no moral principle can be acceptable which holds only for some agents of a certain sort and not for all such agents.[5] I shall call this proposal for a universality test the "minimal universality condition." It seems to pose a problem for the analysis of sets of possible practical principles just given, in that all of the schemata conferring obligations, permissions, etc., on some F's are entailed by the corresponding schemata conferring them on all F's. If the latter are forms of morally acceptable principles of a certain sort, then the former should be so too. Yet the minimal universality test appears to claim that either morally acceptable principles of a certain type, or moral principles in general, cannot have the form "Some F's. . . ." But that test in fact proposes that no morally acceptable principles (and in some versions no moral principles at all) can have the form "Some, but not other similar F's, ..." No principle of the form (R3') "Some, but not other F's, are obliged to do some G act" is entailed by (R1); nor are the corresponding schemata (R4'), (R7'), and (R8') entailed by any of (R1)–(R8). This analysis of the form of practical principles can, therefore, be of use in assessing the minimal universality condition, as well as other proposed universality tests.

Any practical principle which fits schema (1) may also be rendered

[4] R. P. Wolff, *The Autonomy of Reason*, pp. 50–51.

[5] It is put forward by R. M. Hare in *Freedom and Reason* as part of his test for a principle as being a moral one, and is incorporated into his test of rightness by G. M. Singer in *Generalization in Ethics*.

(2) Any (all, none, some) ought to (may, deserve to, etc.) do/omit – – – –
if · · · ·

where "· · · ·" and "– – – –" are, respectively, an agent and an act description. This way of rendering a principle combines the act and agent
descriptions into a single element of the form "– – – – if · · · ·," which is
often convenient. I shall call such combinations of act and agent descriptions
composite act descriptions.

   This form of stating a principle is particularly suitable for expressing the
instantiations of principles that people often adopt, cite, or attribute to others.
The agent descriptions of principles are often omitted and certain agents referred to, either by name or by pronoun, in instantiations of the form

(2) I (she, Billy Graham, Mao Tse-tung, etc.) ought to (may, deserves to
etc.) do/omit – – – – if · · · ·

When agent descriptions are instantiated by replacing them with names or
pronouns, the distinction that practical principles may make between what is
obligatory (permitted, deserved, etc.) for some and for all agents is sub-
merged. There are only four formally different instantiations of (R1)–(R8).
They are

(RI 1) *A* is obliged to do some *G* act.
(RI 2) *A* is not obliged to do any *G* act.
(RI 3) *A* is obliged to refrain from any *G* act.
(RI 4) *A* is not obliged to refrain from any *G* act.

   Act descriptions too may undergo a change in the principles which agents
most often state, cite, or impute to others. These descriptions are often
elided or condensed, a more explicit act description being "understood" as
lying behind the principle cited. A person who cites the principle "Children
ought to behave" is being very inexplicit about the obligations he imputes to
children, but probably has, and is understood as having, something quite
specific in mind. However, act descriptions are not instantiated by names or
definite descriptions of acts, except possibly in judgments about acts that
have already been done, for we do not have names for individual acts that
have not been done.

Some practical principles and instantiations of principles use the verb "will do" rather than one of the compound verbs just listed. "Any club member will pay his dues by March 1" is a practical principle rather than an empirical judgment in its most natural interpretation. The principle "Anyone may enter when he has paid" may sometimes be instantiated by "I shall enter when I have paid"; the principle "Anyone who eats ought not to complain" by "I won't complain when I have eaten." When the main verb of a principle (or instantiation of a principle) is "will," there are only four nonequivalent principles (or instantiations) using a given agent description (or name) and a given act description. Since "will not do" is equivalent to "will omit," the only forms of principles are "All F's will do some G act," "No F's will do any G act," "Some F's will do some G act," and "Some F's will omit any G act." Only two instantiations will use a given name and act description and the verb "will": "A will do some G act" and "A will omit any G act."

We have now examined some of the complexity of the relationship between different practical principles, and between principles and instantiations of principles. A practical principle of form (2) may have its act or its agent description elided or condensed; it may have its agent description elided or even instantiated by a name or definite description; its verb may sometimes be elided in favor of "will do." These elisions and substitutions are important because people very often cite instantiations of principles, or very elliptical principles, rather than explicitly formulated practical principles, which they may nevertheless have "at the back of their minds" and regard as "understood" by others.

Is a universality test to apply to the elliptical principle or instantiation which people cite or to the more explicit principle which is instantiated or condensed? Or can a test on explicit principles discriminate among instantiated and condensed principles? If explicit principles were in one–one or one–many correlation with instantiations and condensed principles this would be possible. But, in fact, the connection is different, as can be seen from a consideration of the (relatively) explicit principle "Any bona fide traveler ought to be served at any hotel." The sentence "John Smith ought to be served at the Red Lion" instantiates not only "Anyone who is a bona fide traveler ought to be served at any hotel" but also indefinitely many other principles, each containing an agent description true of John Smith and an act description true of being served at the Red Lion. Even the apparently fully explicit instantiation of this example, "John Smith ought to be served at the hotel Red Lion if (since) he is a bona fide traveler" instantiates an indefinitely large number of principles.

Even the principle given in this example was not itself fully determinate: it embraced principles such as "Anyone who is a white bona fide traveler ought to be served at any hotel" and "Anyone who is a drunken bona fide traveler ought to be served at any hotel." Nor can principles ever be fully determinate—and if they could, their point as guides to action would be lost, since they would never cover more than a single case. It follows that any instantiation of a principle is an instantiation of many principles, and any principle has many instantiations. Principles and instantiations of principles or condensed versions of principles are in many–many correlation.

Principles, practical or theoretical, are not particulars. They are individuable without reference to location or time. The same is true of instantiations of principles. "I ought to (or will) maximize my expected utility" is an individuable instantiation of the principle "Anybody ought to maximize his expected utility" without any reference to occasions of its adoption. Nor is a linguistic formula or expression for a specific principle or any of its instantiations a particular. But tokens of such expressions for principles and instantiations of principles may be uttered, accepted, or rejected by agents at particular times and places, and are not individuable without spatio-temporal indicators. Each of these tokens of an expression of a specific principle or instantiation of a principle is a particular. The relationship between principles and their instantiations, formulations of principles and of their instantiations, and tokens of these formulations is analogous to that between propositions, sentences, and utterances.

CHAPTER TWO

THE PROBLEM OF
RELEVANT ACT DESCRIPTIONS

✵ I *Principles and Acts*

A universality test is a test of principles, and yet is supposed to help us select acts. If principles and acts were in one–one or one–many correspondence, there would be no problem. We could simply test a principle, and if it turned out that it was morally acceptable (or, more specifically, morally obligatory or morally worthy, etc.), then we would know that any act falling under it would have the same moral status. Unfortunately this is not the case. Not only can a given principle be acted on repeatedly and in various ways, but any given act exemplifies numerous principles. Just as principles and instantiations of principles are in many–many correspondence, so are principles and acts. Of any act and of any agent an indefinitely large number of descriptions is true. So any act is covered by all those principles incorporating at least one true act description and at least one true agent description.

Only if *all* the principles which cover an act meet the condition specified by a universality test, or if *all* of them fail to meet it, can that test of principles be action-guiding. Only in this unusual case would a necessary condition on morally acceptable principles be a necessary condition on an act, or a decision procedure for some species of morally acceptable principles provide one for that sort of morally acceptable act. So if conditions on principles are to be action-guiding, except in this one case, we must specify some way of deciding which of the principles covering an act it is relevant to assess in a given context. We must find some method for deciding what the relevant descriptions of a given agent and act are. Let us call the problem of finding a method by which to select two such descriptions and in doing so to arrive at a single relevant composite act description, the *problem of relevant descriptions*. This is a problem which cannot be avoided by any theory which proposes a condition on principles and claims to be action-guiding. Indeed, it is widely perceived as a crucial problem for which a solution must be provided.

Kant's universality test includes an explicit solution to the problem of relevant descriptions. The principle or instantiation of a principle whose universality it is relevant to test is the one on which the agent acts or proposes to act on a given occasion. This principle or instantiation is the agent's *maxim*. It is Kant's contention that when an act is morally acceptable (in either of two distinct, but clearly defined, ways) the agent's maxim must be a principle of a particular sort. The Categorical Imperative both states a condition on principles and also instructs us as to which principle or instantiation of a principle we should assess in any given context. It incorporates a solution to the problem of relevant descriptions.

An agent's maxim is a particular. Unlike principles and instantiations of principles, it can be individuated only by referring to a person, and so to a place and a time.

It is true that the principle or instantiation which is the content of an agent's maxim is not a particular. But this no more prevents his maxim being a particular than the fact that the sentence "The world is round" is not a particular prevents my belief that the world is round from being one. Propositions, principles, and their instantiations are not particulars; nor are the sentences which state them. But adoptions, assertions, and holdings of propositions, principles, and their instantiations, including maxims, are particulars.

The conditions on morally acceptable principles which we are going to discuss are meant to be action-guiding. To see whether they can be so we must be clear about the relation between principles of various sorts and acts. Acts and maxims are both particulars. But the relation between them is, as stated, a one–many rather than a one–one correlation, and this for two reasons. The first is that some maxims may be acted on repeatedly. I may adopt the maxim "I will rise at 6:00 in the morning" and act on it for more than a single morning. The second reason the relation between maxims and acts is one–many is that there is an indefinite number of ways in which a person can act on a given maxim. I can act on my maxim of early rising cheerfully or reluctantly, fast or slow, by lamplight or in the dark, alone or with others. Even though any of these details might be incorporated into my maxim, there would always remain an area within which the act could vary. Maxims, like principles, cannot be fully determinate.

One type of case suggests that the correlation between maxims and acts may, like that between principles and acts, be many–many rather than one–many. This is the case where agents intentionally kill two or more birds with one stone. A person might shelter from a storm in a shop where he buys his groceries and avoids meeting a creditor on the street. Such cases of multiple or compound maxims may raise a problem of relevant descriptions for Kant's theory. But for standard cases he has a solution. To the extent that the Categorical Imperative is able to discriminate among maxims it will generally be able to discriminate among acts. But the situation is different for those universality tests that apply to entities which are in many–many correlation with acts.

II Two Recent Universality Tests

Recently a number of writers have proposed universality tests which differ from Kant's. Two of the best known are Hare's and Singer's, and they have been extensively discussed during the last decade. I shall not examine the entire ethical theories of Hare and Singer here, nor survey the critical literature, but shall try to appraise their solutions to the problem of relevant descriptions. How is it that each of them hopes to make a universality test on principles action-guiding, even though principles are in many–many correlation with acts?

HARE'S THEORY: FORMALITY WITHOUT FERTILITY. In *Freedom and Reason* Hare proposes a universality test which states a condition, not on principles or on maxims, but on *judgments.* "Moral judgments are a kind of prescriptive judgment, and they are distinguished from other judgments of this class by being universalizable." [1] But a necessary and sufficient condition on moral judgments yields only a necessary condition on the narrower class of morally acceptable judgments. Ethics, according to Hare, is morally neutral. [2]

In this he differs from most proponents of universality tests, who have wanted to use them to demarcate the class of morally acceptable judgments (or principles or acts) or some subset thereof, and so have not thought ethics

[1] R. M. Hare, *Freedom and Reason,* p. 4.   [2] *Ibid.,* p. 97.

morally neutral. But in the end Hare differs less from these other writers than it seems at first. He holds that moral arguments can usually be resolved by rational means. Moral disagreement is rare in practice. What passes as such is usually due to one disputant making not a moral but some other sort of judgment. So a necessary and sufficient condition on the class of moral judgments can, in conjunction with other factors, be an effective, if not decisive, method for determining which judgments are morally acceptable.

If Hare's universality test is to be at all action-guiding, then he must have some solution to the problem of relevant descriptions. But a test on judgments can discriminate among acts only if judgments and acts are in one–many correspondence. A consideration of Hare's use of the term "judgment" shows that this is not the case. The term "judgment" may be taken in various senses. Two are relevant in this context. A judgment is, first, a principle or instantiation of a principle which may (or may not) be used, adopted, or acted on by an agent or another on various occasions. In this sense we may speak of the judgment that anyone who sins must suffer, the judgment that some who eat may complain, or that Caesar was right to cross the Rubicon. In the second relevant sense a judgment is an act of judging, a decision or appraisal, depending on whether the context is one of choice or of assessment. In this sense of judgment we speak of St. Paul's judgment that anyone who sins must suffer or of Caesar's judgment that he would cross the Rubicon, or of my judgment that today's soup is too salty.

These two sorts of judgment are closely connected, yet quite distinct. To decide or appraise is to select a principle or instantiation of a principle (though not all decisions and appraisals are verbally formulated to reveal this). Decisions, assessments, appraisals, and the like are particulars attached to given agents or appraisers at given times, but neither principles nor their instantiations are particulars, though they may be the content of particular mental acts. Particular judgments made by agents and appraisers at given times may contain principles or instantiations of principles which may be of various logical forms. So we can have particular judgments of, for example, universal form or of singular form. Some examples can illustrate this. "Anyone may enter if he pays" is a principle of universal form; "Joe Smith may enter if he pays" is an instantiation of that principle of singular form; Joe Smith's belief "I may enter if I pay" and Bill Brown's belief "Joe Smith may enter if he pays" are particular judgments of singular form and their beliefs that anyone may enter if he pays are particular judgments of universal form.

In most contexts of action and appraisal, people will make judgments of singular form referring to the case at hand. The class of maxims is not coextensive with the class of particular judgments, but with the subset thereof consisting of particular judgments made by agents.

This ambiguity in the term "judgment" is apparent in Hare's ethical theory. The term "judgment" is used, he claims,[3] as a technical term for whatever sentences express, be it statement or not. From this it appears that Hare's sense of "judgment" is that in which the term can be applied to practical principles as well as to propositions. This conclusion is borne out by one of his principal arguments for his universality condition's claim to be part of a necessary and sufficient condition on moral judgments.

Hare holds that moral judgments must be universal because they are a species of descriptive judgment, and so contain descriptive predicates. But descriptive predicates are correctly applied to a given x only if they apply also to all relevantly similar x's. Hence, any judgment applying a descriptive predicate, whether or not it is like a moral judgment and also carries "other sorts of meaning," applies its predicate correctly only if the predicate is also applied to all relevantly similar cases. No moral judgment can have the form "A, but not relevantly similar persons, will (may, ought) – – – –." Moral judgments must be universal in this minimal sense.

This argument suggests that the judgments of which Hare is speaking are principles rather than any sort of act. Predicates are components of judgments in the sense of principles or propositions, but they are not components of acts. But the conclusion that Hare, in fact, claims is not simply that moral principles cannot be of the form "A, but not relevantly similar persons, will (ought, may) – – – – if . . . ." Rather he claims that "a person who makes a moral judgment commits himself to a substantial moral principle." [4] In this context a judgment appears to be not a principle but a decision or appraisal, an act which commits us to an instantiation of a principle or to a principle. We can "make" judgments only if judgments are decisions or appraisals; we cannot make principles. But while it follows, if Hare's argument about descriptive predicates is correct, that the truth of instantiations of principles presupposes the truth of certain principles, it does not follow, given the nature of intensional objects, that making a particular judgment of singular form entails or presupposes making some judgment of universal form.

The root of Hare's ambiguous use of "judgment" is that he wishes to as-

---

[3] *Ibid.,* p. 10.   [4] *Ibid.,* pp. 30, 49, 53, 89.

sert that one and the same thing is *prescriptive* and *universal*. But prescriptivity cannot be predicated of principles, but only of particular holdings, adoptions, or applications of principles or of their instantiations, i.e., of particular judgments. Universality, on the other hand, cannot be predicated of acts of judgment, but only of principles, i.e., of the content of some acts of judgment. Particular judgments may correctly be said to be universally prescribable or universalizable—but this is just to claim that they are related in a specified way to principles of minimally universal form.

It is not hard to reformulate Hare's argument from analogy with descriptive judgments to eliminate any ambiguity in the use of the term "judgment." The reformulation is more complex than the original statement of the argument; it states and seeks to justify a condition on particular moral judgments. Hare could argue not simply that the truth of any descriptive proposition of singular form entails the truth of some descriptive proposition of universal form ("This piece of furniture is a table" entails "Anything relevantly similar to this piece of furniture is a table"), but that, because of this entailment, descriptive judgments of singular form commit one on pain of irrationality to descriptive judgments of minimally universal form. The sense in which they commit is not that an agent who makes a descriptive judgment of singular form must explicitly make some corresponding judgment of universal form, but that he must at least assent to the latter if he understands and attends to it. Descriptive judgments are actually universalized by agents and appraisers who consider and understand their universal counterparts and who are not irrational.

Then, relying on Hare's contention that moral judgments are a species of descriptive judgment, it would follow that agents and appraisers of acts making would-be moral judgments of singular form were committed, in the weak sense just explicated, to some judgment of minimally universal form, or else to being judged irrational. Our moral judgments, too, must be not merely universalizable, but actually universalized by those who understand and attend to their universal counterparts and are not irrational. We must assent to their holding for all relevantly similar cases.

This reformulation should make it clear that Hare's universalizability thesis is in no way trivial, contrary to some recent claims. He is not just arguing that "moral principles must be universal in the trivial sense of applying to everyone and everything that they apply to." [5] He is arguing that

[5] D. Locke, "The Trivializability of Universalizability," *Philosophical Review*, LXXVII (1968), 39–40.

those who use instantiations of such principles in moral judgments *do* or *would* (given attention and understanding), and not merely *could,* assent to their counterparts of universal form. If they don't, their judgments are not moral judgments.

However, Hare has provided only one step toward a solution to the problem of relevant descriptions. Particular judgments are not correlated one–one or one–many with acts, since different persons may make different particular judgments about acts. Hare does not, as Kant does, claim that the agent's judgment, i.e., the maxim of the act, has any special claim to be considered relevant. Of the many particular judgments which may be made about a particular act we need to know which one should be universally prescribed. If this test is to yield action-guiding results, we must pick upon one particular judgment: perhaps the agent's, perhaps that of some qualified other, perhaps that most commonly agreed to. Otherwise universal prescriptivism will not be action-guiding.

For universal prescriptivism does not require that agents assent to the universal counterpart of their maxims, but that *any* person making a particular judgment assent to the universal counterpart of that judgment. Its capacity to resolve moral disagreement is therefore dependent upon the extent to which everyone—agent and spectators alike—can be brought to agree in their particular judgments about an act. It is possible that an agent and other persons might, while all meeting the demands of universal prescriptivism, make conflicting judgments about a certain act.

These points about the relationship between acts, maxims, judgments, and principles can be exhibited by a simple diagram.

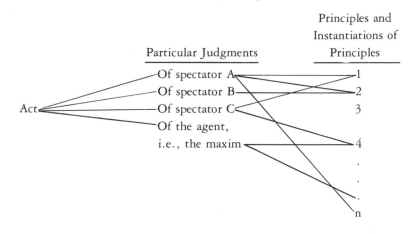

The relationships between particular judgments and principles will, in general, be of great complexity, but it will never be a single one—one or one—many correspondence. Hence, Hare was right to look for a universality condition on judgments rather than principles, for only a condition on particular judgments could be action-guiding. But as the diagram clearly shows, no condition on particular judgments will be action-guiding unless it picks out the judgment of one person as the relevant one to test.

Hare does not deny the possibility of persons making conflicting judgments about an act. After all, he claims that universal prescriptivism cannot resolve all moral disagreement, that it is meant to be ethically neutral and to delimit the class of moral judgments rather than a class of morally acceptable judgments. Nevertheless, he thinks that in actual moral arguments various constraints of context will enable universal prescriptivity to act as a very powerful necessary condition on morally acceptable acts, leaving few moral arguments unresolved or terminating in intuitively unacceptable conclusions. The gap between a necessary condition on moral judgments and a necessary condition on morally acceptable acts can be filled by the constraints of context.

The power of universal prescriptivity in moral arguments is revealed when we remember that a considerable proportion of apparently irresolvable moral arguments are really due to failure to agree on the facts of the case or failure to apply the test of universal prescriptivity imaginatively.[6] Imagination is required in any application of the test if a person is to be sure that he has seriously considered what it would be like to be in the other man's position, so that he can be sure that he is genuinely assenting to a universal principle, which might in another case require him to make a singular judgment with unpleasant implications for himself.[7] If universal prescriptivism is imaginatively applied in the full knowledge of the facts of the case, it will rarely fail to resolve moral disagreement, since people's tastes are on the whole not ec-

---

[6] R. M. Hare, p. 94.

[7] Parts of Hare's argument on the need for imagination in applying universal prescriptivity suggests that he introduces into his ethical theory a variant of the moral point of view—an idealized moral agent who is "prepared to give weight to A's inclinations and interests as if they were his own" (*ibid.*, p. 94). But it seems that Hare does not mean to supersede his earlier and more modest devices. His ideal agent is not endowed with any epistemological or rational capacities, but merely with dispassionate sympathy. It is a device for showing how universal prescriptivity must be applied, rather than an independent touchstone for the morality of acts.

centric.[8] Moral arguments are all *ad hominem,* but nevertheless seldom un-decidable.

The power of such constraints of context to bring arguments about the moral acceptability of acts to conclusions may be admitted, but they are not nearly as decisive as Hare suggests. Though people's taste is seldom eccentric (a matter simply of the meaning of "eccentric"), yet their tastes and desires commonly differ. But these differences need not, Hare thinks, lead to any breakdowns in moral argument. When two persons come to conflicting moral judgments, the conflict may often be resolved by showing that, at a more general level of act description, one judgment is reversed.[9] For ex-ample, a man who is willing to assent to the universal judgment "Anyone may play the trumpet whenever he wishes" may not be willing to assent to the universal judgment "Anyone may inconvenience his neighbor by making noise when he wishes."

But this move is not going to produce the results which Hare hopes for. People are willing to universalize some but not others of the more general particular judgments they make about a given act. In Hare's example while many persons will not agree to universalize the judgment that one may in-convenience neighbors with noise, many will agree to universalize judg-ments such as "I should develop my talents" or "I should take advantage of cultural opportunities." Only an implicit theory of moral relevance (a utili-tarian one, perhaps) could lead Hare to regard the refusal to prescribe univer-sally "One may inconvenience neighbors with noise" as able to decide the argument about trumpet playing.

On the whole, the move of shifting to a more general description of an act to show that some assessment of an act is mistaken backfires as often as it helps resolve moral arguments. Does it help us to decide whether it is per-missible to mislead the police in their pursuit of a friend suspected of crime to note that most of us are willing to prescribe universally the judgment "I ought to help my friends" and that most of us are not willing to prescribe universally the judgment "I shall obstruct justice"?

It was to avoid just this sort of problem in assessing the moral accept-ability of acts that I have insisted that no ethical theory requiring but lack-ing a solution to the problem of relevant descriptions can be acceptable. We may be able to "appeal" to a more general act description; but not all the results of such appeals will bring moral arguments to a close, and even those that do end an argument may do so without justification. What we need to

[8] *Ibid.,* pp. 111, 171–73.   [9] *Ibid.,* pp. 113–96.

know is when such appeals are justified. We need to know what to do, and not just what the procedural features of deciding morally are.

Hare does not regard this as a problem. Indeed, he admits that even when the various constraints of context are taken into account—the need for imagination, the general agreement of tastes, the possibility when this is lacking of appealing to a more general act description—his ethical theory may yet produce some surprising moral assessments of acts. He does not suggest reasons why the constraints of context should resolve a conflict between moral judgments in favor of the one which is morally acceptable. When an agent is committed to a universal judgment enjoining some act regardless of other considerations, then no appeal to a different, more general act description is likely to be accepted, given the agent's reluctance to universalize a principle incorporating it.

Hare describes such an agent as having *ideals*.[10] Ideals cannot be shown wrong by appeal to the agent's or another's inclinations and interests, for disregard of these is built into any ideal. Hence, no act done in the name of an ideal can be shown morally unacceptable by the pattern of moral argument Hare proposes. For this reason Hare calls the determined holder of an ideal a fanatic.

Universal prescriptivism cannot show that when a fanatic acts in the name of his ideal his judgment or his act is morally unacceptable. Fanatics may be universal prescriptivists, and the theory has no method of showing some ideal perverted. But even so, Hare argues once again, this is in practice a minor difficulty. In the context of particular moral arguments, things will on the whole operate against the fanatic and for the liberal (the man whose ideal is that of allowing all to pursue their ideals if they do not interfere with others). Most fanaticism is the product of confusion—of insufficient attention to facts or belief in spurious "facts," or of lack of imagination. It is rare for a man to hold a "perverted" universal principle which overrides all other considerations and to be totally clear about what he is doing. So universal prescriptivism is not, even on Hare's reckoning, sufficient to resolve moral disagreements. Though there is no universally decisive pattern of moral argument, once moral ideals are involved, most moral arguments will be decided—in favor of the liberals.[11] Unfortunately it does not follow that they will be decided in favor of those acts which are morally acceptable.

[10] *Ibid.*, p. 176.
[11] *Ibid.*, ch. 8 and ch. 9, pp. 137–85. Hare's reading of history, with which he buttresses the argument summarized here, is highly selective. No doubt illiberal

With the move from principles to particular judgments Hare's theory took a step in the direction of a solution to the problem of relevant descriptions. But he did not reach a solution. The particular judgments of different persons about an act commonly differ, and he has no method for singling out one judgment as relevant for the test of universal prescriptivism. Constraints of context may eliminate some moral disagreements, but not as many as Hare supposes. Even when moral disagreement happens to be absent, we have no grounds for supposing that the results are morally preferable to other positions which are rejected, for even a consensus may be iniquitous. Universal prescriptivism is sometimes not action-guiding at all, and is least likely to be so in situations where disagreements are deep and guidance most needed. Even when it guides we have slender grounds for believing that it must lead to morally acceptable acts. Universal prescriptivism delineates a formal condition on moral judgment, but is a barren theory.

SINGER'S THEORY: FERTILITY WITHOUT FORMALITY. In *Generalization in Ethics* Singer uses a principle very similar to Hare's for an entirely different purpose. He states a universality test, which he calls the *generalization principle,* as follows:

GP What is right (or wrong) for one person must be right (or wrong) for any similar person in similar circumstances.[12]

Like Hare's use of the minimal universality test, this condition implies that no principle of right can have the form *"A,* but not those relevantly similar, ought. . . ."* But the differences between Hare's and Singer's use of minimal universality are considerable.

Singer hopes that the condition will help to demarcate, not the class of moral principles in general, but that subclass of moral principles which consists of *acceptable* principles of *right.* (The latter restriction is not important in Singer's ethical theory: the only moral principles of which he talks are principles of right.) Minimal universality is not a sufficient condition of a principle's being an acceptable principle of right, though it is necessary. To make

---

ideals have been pursued without clear thinking on many occasions. So have liberal ones. The evidence that clear-headed universal prescriptivism will lead people to reject all but liberal ideals is rather slight.

[12] M. G. Singer, p. 5.

his theory action-guiding, Singer has therefore to add other conditions to minimal universality. This he does by combining minimal universality with a utilitarian principle into a *generalization argument*. The argument has this form:

GA If everyone were to do *x,* the consequences would be disastrous (or un-desirable); therefore no one has the right to do *x.*

The argument is, Singer claims, based on the combination of a *principle of consequences,* namely

PC If the consequences of *A*'s doing *x* would be undesirable, then *A* has no right to do *x.*

and of his minimal universality condition, GP.[13]

The arguments presented to buttress these contentions are slender. The generalization principle is said to be "presupposed in every genuine moral judgment" and "an essential part of the meaning of such moral terms as 'right,' 'wrong,' and 'ought' in their distinctively moral senses." [14] This justification is reminiscent of Hare's claim that any judgment not universally prescribed cannot be moral. In each case, too much depends on the sense ascribed to "moral," and it is hard to find arguments showing exactly what may legitimately be built into that term, whether it is taken in the broader sense Hare intends, or in the narrower sense with which Singer is usually concerned.

The principle of consequences is justified as being "a necessary ethical or moral principle," both in the sense that "its denial involves self-contradiction" and in the sense that it is a "necessary presupposition or precondition of all moral reasoning." [15] These claims are not obviously true, and would also, once again, be justified only if a great deal can be built into the term "moral." However, I am concerned here not so much with Singer's justification of his principles as with their power to discriminate. Singer claims that they have such powers. Granted the principle of consequences and the generalization principle, he claims that the generalization argument follows. We may, then, move from PC to a *generalized principle of consequences* of the form

---

[13] Cf. *Ibid.,* ch. 4 for various formulations of these principles.
[14] *Ibid.,* p. 34.   [15] *Ibid.,* p. 64.

GC If the consequences of everyone's doing x would be undesirable, then it
is not the case that everyone has the right to do x.

From this it is said to follow that if the consequences of everybody's doing x
would be undesirable, some people have no right to do x, and hence by GP,
that nobody has the right to do x. The generalization argument is a necessary
and sufficient condition on acceptable principles of right.[16]

The most damaging charge against GA is not that its justification is shaky
(that might be remediable), but that unless supplemented with a solution to
the problem of relevant descriptions, it is vulnerable to countless arguments
of *reductio ad absurdum* form. If nobody has the right to do an act which
would have unfortunate consequences if everybody did it, then there can be
few acts which anybody has the right to do. Sitting or standing at a particular spot, working as a middleman (or artist, or engine driver, or not at all),
borrowing or lending money, belonging to an intimate club, and countless
other acts would not be permissible. In some cases neither doing nor refraining from doing a certain act would be permissible. It would be wrong either
to do or not to do such acts. Singer is aware of these difficulties, and gives
the example of growing food, which, he says, would lead to unfortunate consequences if done by everybody or by nobody. Applications of GA which
show that it is wrong both to do x and not to do x are said by Singer to be
invertible. Such applications of GA lead to logically unacceptable consequences; many others such as some of the above examples lead to intuitively
unacceptable consequences.

The problems which arise when GA is applied are again a consequence of
lacking a solution to the problem of relevant descriptions. Those cases where
nobody is willing to conclude that all acts of some sort are wrong because everybody's doing them that would have unfortunate consequences are ones in
which some but not all subsets of the acts are wrong. For instance, refusing

---

[16] Singer gives a variety of formulations of each of GP, PC, GC, GA. Some
formulations are not equivalent to other formulations of the same principle. From
some formulations of the first three and perhaps all, no formulation of GA can be
validly derived. Since I am not chiefly concerned with questions of justifiability, I
shall neglect the detail of controversy surrounding Singer's deduction. Given how
shaky the justifications for GP and PC are, there is little doubt that GA has not been
justified. But there is no need to overkill that unfortunate principle here. Each of the
principles has been stated here in a form which seems to accord with Singer's intentions.

to work except as an engine driver when there are no openings and other jobs are available might be wrong if one needed a job to support one's family; growing food might be wrong in those cases where it merely contributes to a glut and impoverishes the farmer's family. But in other circumstances both growing food and refusing to work except as an engine driver might well neither of them be wrong.

Singer uses a variety of *ad hoc* devices to discriminate between the sort of act description which makes an act wrong, and the sort which does not. But he does not try to give any general solution to the problem of relevant descriptions. Rather he concentrates on some special cases of the problem and tries to hedge GA with restrictions which will prevent its leading to unacceptable conclusions.

The main restriction he proposes is that GA can show an act to be wrong only if it does not show the omission of that act to be wrong. When an application of the GA is invertible, it can show the act as described neither right nor wrong, but only *morally indeterminate*.[17] The requirement that applications of GA can lead to conclusions about the moral acceptability of acts only if they are not invertible is supposed to eliminate from the class of acceptable principles of right those whose composite act descriptions are "too general."[18] But this restriction is far from solving the problems posed by the fact that any act done by any agent exemplifies many principles with varying composite act descriptions. There is no reason to think that GA will turn out to be invertible with respect to all but one of the composite descriptions of a given act. Usually many descriptions of an act are, in Singer's terms, morally determinate. So GA may yet show, as Singer admits, a single act, variously described, both right and wrong.[19]

Applications of the generalization argument can also mislead when they classify as wrong any act described as done under certain restrictions of time and place. Since acts are particulars and therefore all fall under descriptions which refer to a time and a place, this means that some applications of the GA can be found that will show wrong any act whatsoever, unless the act were one which everyone can do simultaneously at one spot! The difficulty arises in this way. For any sort of act, *x,* there would be undesirable consequences if everybody tried to do it at a particular time and place (overcrowding, neglect of other essential duties, etc.). But if it were wrong to do *x* at each time and place, then there is no time or place when it is not wrong to

[17] M. Singer, p. 76.   [18] *Ibid.*   [19] *Ibid.,* p. 143.

do *x;* hence *x* is wrong *tout court.* In such cases GA is said by Singer to be *reiterable.*[20] The second restriction placed on uses of the generalization argument is that they cannot show an act wrong by being reiterated to show that it would be wrong at each possible time and place. This restriction eliminates from the class of morally acceptable principles those whose act descriptions are "too specific." [21]

But even taking this restriction and the invertibility restriction together, a multiplicity of descriptions of any act which are neither morally indeterminate nor too specific remain. GA could be a fruitful guide to action only if some criterion were available to decide which of the remaining true descriptions of an act are the ones under which it may be enjoined or forbidden on a given class of agents. While this problem is unsolved, the argument form may classify some acts as both right and wrong and may lead to intuitively unacceptable conclusions. It still remains open to countless counter-arguments of *reductio ad absurdum* form.

Singer tries to narrow down further the class of principles which the GA can show morally unacceptable by suggesting that, whenever a principle includes an agent description that individuates a single agent, the GA cannot vindicate the principle's claim to be morally acceptable.[22] This condition is meant to prevent principles whose minimal universality seems spurious (e.g., "Everybody named Ignatz Macgillycuddy . . ."; "Everyone living in this house . . .") from being morally acceptable principles, even though these principles do not violate the minimal universality condition. But this restriction also misses the mark. We do not want to prejudge that no duty or right can belong to a person in virtue of a uniquely individuating description. Yet if we accept Singer's contention that everyone is unique in some respect, so that GA is reiterable with respect to "characteristics selected as unique," [23] this is precisely what we must do. We must suppose that "the founder of Islam" and "the only doctor to have examined the accused" cannot have special right or duties in virtue of these descriptions. Equally we must suppose that if suddenly a host of men were named Ignatz Macgillycuddy then, for some reason, it would now be possible for them to have rights or duties enjoined on them in virtue of their falling under the agent description "named Ignatz Macgillycuddy." Neither of these suppositions is plausible. Whether a principle's universality is legitimate or spurious is indeed an in-

[20] *Ibid.,* p. 81.   [21] *Ibid.,* p. 82.   [22] *Ibid.,* pp. 87 ff.
[23] *Ibid.,* p. 88.

teresting question; but it cannot be answered by seeing how many agents come within the principle's scope.

Singer's attempts to suggest a line of demarcation do not succeed in codifying our intuitions about whether universality is legitimate or not; but he does not show that these intuitions can be discounted. Yet we can hardly presuppose the intuitions in an ethical theory. Some other account is needed. An adequate solution to the problem of relevant descriptions would provide it.

In his various attempts to draw a line between relevant and irrelevant composite act descriptions, Singer eventually suggests that what is important is whether the particular act and agent descriptions incorporated in a given principle refer to characteristics which affect the desirability of the probable consequences of the act.[24] Agent descriptions such as "named Ignatz Macgillycuddy," act descriptions such as "writing" will usually have no bearing on the desirability of the probable consequences of acts of that sort done by agents of that sort. Agent and act descriptions such as "the man who signed the contract to provide concrete" or "murdering" will often have some bearing on the desirability of the probable consequences of acts of that sort or done by agents of that sort. The latter descriptions, but not the former, are (in typical contexts) morally relevant descriptions. They are the sort of descriptions which provide a legitimate basis for assigning rights and duties which one would not assign to agents not meeting the descriptions, for condemning or endorsing acts which one would not condemn or endorse if they could not be so described.

Yet even combining these measures with Singer's other restrictions designed to eliminate principles incorporating either too general or too specific agent descriptions, a problem remains. Many acts may be enjoined on agents (or forbidden them) in virtue of a number of different descriptions, all of which have some bearing on the desirability of the act's probable consequences. A single act may be an instance of lying, of misleading a criminal, of helping a friend or of harming a friend, and of aiding and abetting a murder (imagine that the householder in Kant's well-known example is a friend of the would-be murderer as well as of his intended victim). The desirability of the probable consequences of acts of each of these sorts may differ. The probable consequences of helping a friend might be desirable, those of acts falling under the other descriptions in general undesirable.

[24] *Ibid.*, pp. 89, 139.

Singer contends that this problem is not, in the context of his theory, very formidable.[25] But he fails to state just what its solution is. Indeed he claims that no general solution to the problem is needed, and that in particular cases of competing morally relevant descriptions:

One and the same act can be of a kind that is generally right and also of a kind that is generally wrong. . . . This is frequently the situation when there is a conflict of rules, leading to a moral problem. To describe the act in such a way as to obscure this fact about it is a mistake, and if it is not made honestly, is itself morally wrong.[26]

But how can we tell when and whether we are making the mistake? Once we know that a particular act has several competing morally relevant descriptions, is it simply a matter for intuition to decide under which of these it should be assessed? Or must it be assessed under their conjunction?

Though Singer gives no guidance for such situations, a very natural extension of his theory provides a solution to the problem of relevant descriptions. This solution is suggested by Lyons in *Forms and Limits of Utilitarianism*. In the context of a utilitarian ethical theory any description of an act is morally relevant in virtue of which the act may be expected to have either desirable or undesirable consequences. There are many such descriptions. But only one of these is a *complete* morally relevant description.[27]

Finding the complete morally relevant description of any act is not, as Lyons points out, a mechanical task. An act may have indefinitely many true descriptions in virtue of which its consequences are likely to be either desirable or undesirable. Even if an act had only a definite number of such descriptions, there is no search procedure for listing them. Nor is it a simple matter to decide when any given property of an act is causally relevant, and so, possibly, relevant in determining the desirability of the probable consequences of the act. Some properties may be correlated with desirable or undesirable probable consequences without being the causes of such consequences. To use Lyons' example, acts done on a Tuesday may have more desirable consequences than acts done at other times. But if this is so it is probably not because "done on a Tuesday" is a morally relevant description, since the date on which acts are done is not usually something which determines their effects. It is more likely that being done on a Tuesday is correlated with some other genuinely causal property of acts.

[25] *Ibid.*, p. 144.   [26] *Ibid.*, pp. 144–45; cf. also p. 154.
[27] Cf. D. Lyons, pp. 55–61.

While Lyons' method of selecting the complete morally relevant description of an act is not mechanical, it is still feasible. We can with diligence find many of the most important determinants of the desirability of an act's consequences. Further it is a procedure which it is easy to justify in an ethical theory which includes a utilitarian principle. If the rightness or wrongness of acts depends on the desirability of their probable consequences, then assessments of the rightness of acts should concentrate on those properties of acts in virtue of which they have desirable or undesirable consequences. An act which can be described as x or y or z is relevantly described as x only if none of the more complete descriptions, xy, xz, yz, and xyz, assigns the act to a subset of x's the desirability of whose probable consequences differs from that of x's in general; it is correctly described as xy only if being described as xyz would not assign it to a subset of xy's with probable consequences whose desirability differs from that of xy's in general.

If Singer had adopted this method for selecting the complete morally relevant description of an act, he could have dispensed with the *ad hoc* and collectively insufficient restrictions disallowing applications of GA which are either invertible or reiterable. When an application of the argument is invertible, i.e., when it shows that doing x and refraining from doing x are both wrong, then there must be some x's, say xz's, which are wrong and other x's, say xy's, which are.not wrong. The problem of invertibility does not arise when descriptions are complete. And when an application of GA is reiterable, i.e., when it can be shown that any one of xy_1, xy_2, . . . xy_n is wrong, where any x must be xy_1 or xy_2, etc., and so that x is wrong, though intuitively this is not so, then Lyons' method for generating complete morally relevant descriptions would show that none of y_1, y_2, . . . y_n is a morally relevant description of the act, and so that none of these should appear in the complete morally relevant description of x.

It is therefore open to Singer to adopt a method of finding the complete morally relevant description of an act. It seems that he can avoid the problem which beset Hare's theory. But there is a cost to doing this. Singer could justify adopting Lyons' solution to the problem of relevant descriptions only because he has in any case adopted a utilitarian principle as a fundamental part of his ethical theory. It is all and only those properties of an act which are causally related to its expected desirability which are included in a complete morally relevant description of the act. Hence, this solution to the problem of relevant descriptions is open only to those theorists who are prepared to adopt a utilitarian principle. And there are various reasons for not doing that. Some of these have been mentioned in discussing Singer's failure to supply a convincing justification for his principle of consequences or to lay out his assumptions about measuring desirability. There are also the counterintuitive principles of right to which utilitarian theories may lead, and other familiar difficulties of these sorts. But in the context of assessing various universality tests there is another, fundamental objection to adopting a utilitarian principle. The whole attraction of investigating universality tests lies in their alleged capacity to be fruitful conditions on morally acceptable principles which can be accepted on the basis of very meager, possibly formal, presuppositions. Once we adopt a utilitarian principle we cease to place any weight on a notion of universality. We are committed to a strong value theory and strong assumptions about the measurement of utility. Indeed, if Singer were to adopt Lyons' method for selecting complete morally relevant act descriptions, the minimal universality condition would become a redundant part of his ethical theory. The principle of consequences alone would, if applied only to complete morally relevant descriptions of acts, show right and wrong whole classes of relevantly similar acts. If one completely and relevantly described act, say x, is wrong, then any other act, say y, whose complete relevant description is the same as x's will also be wrong. It will still be true of Singer's ethical theory that principles of right must be minimally universal. No act will be right or wrong for one person and not for another in relevantly similar circumstances. But minimal universality is no longer an independent condition on the moral acceptability of acts.

Lyons' thesis that there is no substantive choice between general and act utilitarianism therefore depends on the adoption of this solution to the problem of relevant descriptions. Only because the complete morally relevant description of an act consists of all and only those descriptions of the act which refer to causal properties likely to affect the act's desirability are the results of asking "Is this particular act right?" and "Are acts of this sort right?" always the same. In criticizing those who have not thought act and general utilitarianism extensionally equivalent, Lyons is therefore criticizing their failure to adopt his solution to the problem of relevant descriptions. Given that no alternative solution has generally been offered, this seems fair enough.

SUMMARY. Several points emerge from this discussion of two recent non-Kantian universality conditions. The most important of these is that the ethical theories built around such conditions have failed to solve the problem of relevant descriptions. They cannot be applied to particular cases of moral assessment to yield determinate results. Singer considered the lack of a solution to the problem of relevant descriptions a serious difficulty for his ethical theory, but did not fill the gap satisfactorily. I have argued that this gap is a very serious problem. We cannot presuppose an intuitive knowledge of which composite act descriptions it is relevant to assess in various contexts in any application of an ethical theory. If that were permissible, we might as well presuppose an intuitive knowledge of the rightness and wrongness of acts, and so dispense for all practical purposes with an ethical theory.

Neither Hare's nor Singer's ethical theory fulfills the promise that many people find in the idea of a universality test. Hare's theory is not generally action-guiding, and even when universal prescriptivists agree in their moral judgments, we do not know whether they will agree in a morally acceptable judgment: formality is maintained at the expense of fertility. Singer's theory has implications for action, but they are reached by swamping the appealing parsimony of a universality test in the bog of utilitarianism. And when his theory is completed by Lyons' solution to the problem of relevant descriptions, its reliance on a universality test is superseded. Fertility is achieved at the expense of formality.

Not surprisingly there appears to be a conflict between the parsimony and the fertility of an ethical theory. Nevertheless, a better balance between the two may be obtainable than either of the theories so far examined has to offer. With this hope I shall now subject Kant's Categorical Imperative to the same sorts of questions as were raised about Hare's and Singer's work in this chapter.

CHAPTER THREE

A SOLUTION TO THE PROBLEM
OF RELEVANT DESCRIPTIONS [1]

The most famous of all universality tests is Kant's Categorical Imperative. He formulates the test in a number of ways and claims that they are equivalent. I shall not examine this claim, but shall concentrate on the main formulation of the test which explicitly uses the notion of universality, but does not explicitly use any of the other central Kantian notions, such as autonomy, treating others as ends, acting as a legislator in the kingdom of ends, and so on. This formulation of the test is the *Formula of Universal Law*. It runs:

I. Act only on that maxim through which you can at the same time will that it should become a universal law.

A second and subsidiary formulation, which also depends on the notion of universality, is the *Formula of the Law of Nature*. It runs:

Ia. Act as if the maxim of your action were to become through your will a universal law of nature.[2]

Some justification is needed for a decision to concentrate on Formulas I and Ia. Many would claim that these are the least interesting, the most sterile and "formalistic" versions of the Categorical Imperative. To concen-

---

[1] In the next three chapters there will be frequent references to Kant's works on ethics. All references will be to the edition of the Prussian Academy of Sciences as described in the Bibliography. The pagination of the Prussian Academy edition is given in the margins of each of these translations, and it alone is used for all references.

[2] The formulas are quoted in the versions in which they appear at *G.*, p. 421. The numbering is Paton's. Cf. H. J. Paton, *The Moral Law*, and H. J. Paton, *The Categorical Imperative*, especially p. 129.

trate on these, it is said, is to miss the humanistic core of Kant's ethics, and attention should rather be paid to the notions of autonomy, treating others as ends, acting as a legislator, and so on. I have two reasons for disregarding such advice. First, I do not believe that Formulas I and Ia are sterile. Chapter 5 will show the extent to which they can be action-guiding. Second, the formalism, such as it is, of these two formulas is one of their merits. It is easier to work out the implications of (relatively) formal requirements than of other sorts of requirements. If Formulas I and Ia lead nowhere, it should at least be possible to determine this quite precisely. These formulas are, Kant says, the "strictest" versions of the Categorical Imperative, though others may be more useful for securing acceptance of the moral law.[3]

Many readers will view this attempt to connect formalism with what is humanly and morally interesting and important with scepticism. The formalism of Kant's ethics is often thought incompatible with a concern with human ends. Recent, and indeed not-so-recent, articles and books on Kant's ethics will reveal many variants of this view. There are writers who claim that Kant proposes a formal criterion for morality and consequently reaches substantive ethical conclusions which are not humanly interesting, either because they are (in one version) trivial or because (in another version) they are harshly abstract and "rigoristic." Such writers often ignore everything Kant says about ends. On the other hand, some commentators credit Kant with a theory of human ends but believe that he holds it at the expense of contradicting his own commitment to formalism and to avoiding heteronomy. The rehearsal of these charges is as wearisome as that battlefield of endless controversies called metaphysics,[4] and I hope to settle the issue.

Since I am concerned with showing that Formulas I and Ia can be used effectively to perform certain tasks, my discussion of Kant's ethical theory has to be extremely selective. In particular, I shall not discuss systematically Kant's derivation of particular duties either in the *Grundlegung* or in the *Metaphysik der Sitten*. For most of these derivations do not in fact make use of either Formula I or Formula Ia. Kant's arguments are often extremely sketchy and appeal to *The Formula of the End in Itself* (especially in the second part of the *Metaphysik der Sitten*) or to various "natural purposes" (the natural purpose of sex being procreation, that of self-love the preservation of life, and so on). To show that the stricter formulas are not practically useless, it is necessary to connect Kant's classification of duties with them, and this can be

---

[3] *G.,* p. 436.   [4] Cf. *Critique of Pure Reason,* A viii.

done only by taking all the clues he gives, while disregarding irrelevant derivations. Although this chapter and the next one will be closer to exegesis than the rest of the book, they will not be, and are not supposed to be, a detailed textual commentary.

Formulas I and Ia both prescribe a universality test on maxims as a method for determining the moral acceptability of acts. First, I shall consider in greater detail than was possible in chapter 2 just what Kant's maxims are and whether they provide a solution to the problem of relevant descriptions. Many writers deny that Kant has solved this problem.[5]

I Maxims, Ends, and Intentions

A maxim is in the first place a practical principle, differentiated from other practical principles by the fact that it is the principle of a particular rational agent at a particular time.[6] Kant expresses this by calling maxims *subjective principles,* thus distinguishing them from *objective principles* or *practical laws,* which are valid for all rational agents at all times, but will not always be adopted by any but wholly rational agents—beings who have what Kant calls a holy will. The aim of the test stated by the Categorical Imperative is to show which maxims conform to practical laws. Any maxim that does conform is a *maxim of duty* for any finite rational agent; a maxim that does not conform is a *mere maxim.*[7] For principles which are practical laws we may construct counterparts in the imperative mood which Kant refers to as cate-

[5] Some of Kant's commentators have taken the term "maxim" as being synonymous with "principle," and have charged him with failing to offer any solution to the problem of relevant descriptions. Cf. D. Ross, *Kant's Ethical Theory,* pp. 32–33; T. C. Williams, *The Concept of the Categorical Imperative,* pp. 54–55; A. C. Ewing, "The Paradoxes of Kant's Ethics," *Philosophy,* XIII (1938), p. 49.

[6] For this and subsequent definitions and distinctions, cf. *K.P.V.,* p. 19 ff. and *G.,* pp. 400 *n.,* 413–25, especially p. 421 *n.*

[7] Cf. *K.P.V.,* p. 19; also L. W. Beck, *A Commentary on Kant's Critique of Practical Reason,* pp. 75–84. There are some difficulties with the passage. Beck (p. 81) regards the maxim/practical law distinction as "logically faulty" since laws are a subspecies of maxim. But this is not so, since some laws may never be adopted as maxims by any agent. Rather the trouble is that some practical principles are laws (and of these some may at some times be adopted as maxims); some principles are at some times adopted as maxims, without being laws ("mere" maxims), and some principles are neither laws nor (at any time) adopted as maxims. The latter might be called "possible mere maxims."

gorical imperatives.[8] Kant's reason for distinguishing the imperative counterparts of practical laws is that these principles are experienced as imperatives by finite rational agents such as men, who are not immediately inclined
to adopt these principles and so feel a measure of constraint when they do
choose to adopt them.

Maxims, being practical principles or instantiations of such principles,
may be rendered schematically either by

(2) Any (all, none, some) ought to (may, deserves to, etc.) do/omit $----$ if
$\cdots$

or by

(2′) I (he, X) ought to (may, deserves to, etc.) do/omit $----$ if $\cdots$

Since maxims are often adopted for personal use only, they may be very ellip-
tically formulated. All specification of the agent and even of whether the act
is thought to be obligatory or permitted or to have some other status may
often be eliminated as "understood," and the maxim rendered schematically
simply by

(3) To $----$ if $\cdots$,

or by

(3′) I will $----$ if $\cdots$,

where "$----$" and "$\cdots$" are as before filled, respectively, by some act
description and some agent description and form together a composite act
description. The imperative counterpart of a given maxim would have the
form

[8] The name of the "supreme principle of morality" is "the Categorical Imperative," and will be capitalized throughout, as will the names of its various formulations. The imperative counterparts of principles meeting the requirements of the Categorical Imperative are categorical imperatives. Similarly the imperative counterparts
of principles which meet the requirements of the Principle of Hypothetical Imperatives are hypothetical imperatives.

$(3'')$ $- - - -$ if $\cdots$.

If the Categorical Imperative were in a strict sense a formal test on maxims (or on imperatives), then one would expect it to state certain conditions for the instantiation of these schemata, which must be met if the maxim is to be a practical law. It ought in that case to be possible to decide from the most cursory inspection of an agent's maxim whether it was a practical law or a mere maxim. But nothing in Kant's writing, except his unfortunate, though dramatic, use of the term "categorical" in the name he gives to his universality test and to the imperative counterparts of maxims which meet that test, suggests that the Categorical Imperative proposes so simple a test on maxims.

By using the word "categorical" Kant suggests that objective principles should be of categorical (rather than, say, of hypothetical or of disjunctive) form. This would mean that any maxim whose agent description component was not void would be a mere maxim, while any maxim whose agent description component was void would be a practical law. Every maxim lacking an agent description would have an imperative counterpart of categorical form. But this is clearly not Kant's intention. "Shut the door" is not a categorical imperative; "If you have promised, keep your promise" presumably is. But only the former and the maxim corresponding to it are of categorical form. The form which categorical imperatives, and so practical laws, must have is determined by the test stated in Formula I of the Categorical Imperative, and has nothing to do with the categorical form which propositions may have.[9]

The degree of specificity or generality of the act and agent descriptions of the examples of maxims that Kant gives varies enormously. His examples include the following: "From self-love to shorten my life whenever its continuance threatens more evil than it promises pleasure" [10]; "Whenever I

[9] Cf., e.g., L. W. Beck, "Apodictic Imperatives," *Kant-Studien*, Vol. 49, 1957, pp. 7, 17 ff., and M. Moritz, *Kant's Einteilung der Imperative, passim*. Beck suggests that because of the misleading suggestions of the term "categorical" we should use the phrase "apodictic imperatives" to refer to the imperative counterparts of practical laws, pp. 20–22. Though Kant does sometimes use the term "apodictic imperative," I shall continue to use the customary term "categorical imperative," in the full realization that the class of categorical imperatives is not a class of imperatives whose form is categorical. See also M. G. Singer, ch. 8, pp. 217–38, on this topic.

[10] *G.*, p. 422.

believe myself short of money, I will borrow money and promise to pay it back though I know that this will never be done"; [11] and "To promote according to his means the happiness of others who are in need, and this without the hope of gaining anything by it." [12] Despite the varying degrees of generality in these specimen maxims, there is clearly a limit to the amount of detail about an agent's circumstances and his proposed act which can be included in his maxims. Subsidiary rules may incorporate some of these. But even these cannot multiply to take account of the entire profusion of possible circumstances. Applying a maxim and one of its subsidiary rules always requires an exercise of judgment. In this maxims share the liabilities—and advantages—of all practical principles.

As the first of the specimen maxims shows, the agent's maxim may include not only an act and an agent description, but also a *purposive component*. This does not show that not all maxims fit the schemata suggested, for the purposive component can be regarded as an amplification of the act description. In some contexts it is essential to consider an agent's purposes explicitly, and in these cases the agent's maxim may be rendered schematically by

(4) To − − − − if · · · · in order to ——,

where "——" is filled by some specification of the agent's purpose in acting. Any element of the form "− − − − if · · · · in order to ——" will be called an *amplified act description*. Since Kant believes that all human action is purposive [13] any maxim may be stated in sufficient detail to fit into the schematic form (4). The first of the specimen maxims, for instance, would be rendered "To shorten my life if its continuance threatens more evil than it promises pleasure, in order to achieve that I want." [14] But the purposive component of an agent's maxim does not have to refer to some further purpose of the agent. I may go for a walk either to enjoy the spring sunshine or just to go for a walk. So there can be maxims whose form is

(4') To — − − − if · · · · in order to − − − − if · · · ·

[11] *Ibid.*   [12] *M.S.*, p. 453. This is the "maxim of beneficence."
[13] *M.S.*, p. 384.
[14] Kant terms any act whose purpose is some end desired by the agent an act of self-love. Cf. chapter 6, section III, for a more extensive account of his theories of motives and of ends.

What I have called the purposive component of an agent's maxim might also be regarded as a statement of the agent's motive, in one sense of that much debated term. It is in this sense that Kant uses the term "motive." An agent's motive is not, for Kant, simply some sort of emotion or feeling. It is that for which an agent does any act. Acts done to achieve some desired end are all done with the motive of achieving what is desired, i.e., out of self-love. The more specific motives falling under the general heading of self-love are all what Kant calls *empirical motives* or *inclinations.* Acts done to realize whatever end or ends duty may demand are all said to be done with a *pure motive.* The important point at this stage is that pure and empirical motives are not psychological states or proclivities which may be attributed to an agent whatever his ends. Kant's theory of motives is a mirror image of his theory of ends.

Though all maxims have a purposive component, there are many contexts of moral assessment in which Kant regards this as irrelevant. In such cases we abstract from ends and consider the agent's maxim in, say, form (3). But there are other moral contexts in which it is necessary to consider the purposive component of an agent's maxim. Following a usage Kant suggests but does not develop, I shall call maxims whose purposive component is suppressed *maxims of action,* and those whose purposive component is expressed (whether or not the rest of the agent's maxim is made explicit) *maxims of ends.*[15] When an agent's maxims of action and of ends are fully expressed, in an amplified act description, as in (4), I shall call his maxim a *complete maxim of ends.* When the composite act description is suppressed and we know the agent's proposed ends, but not his means, I shall call his maxim an *incomplete maxim of ends.* Incomplete maxims of ends have the form

(4″) To do/omit what is needed in order to ———.

Formula I of the Categorical Imperative can be applied to maxims of either sort; but depending on which application is being undertaken, the formula can be stated in either of two restricted ways. When the application of the formula to maxims of action is under consideration, it may be expressed "act externally in such a way that the free use of your power of choice is compatible with the freedom of everyone according to a universal law."

[15] *M.S.,* p. 395.

This is the "Universal Principle of Justice." [16] When the application of the formula to a maxim of ends is under consideration, it can be stated in the restricted form "Act according to a maxim of ends which can be a universal law for everyone to have." This is the "First Principle of the Doctrine of Virtue." [17] The relation between Formula I and these two subsidiary formulas is simple enough and will be substantiated in chapters 4 and 5. Formula I concerns maxims in general; the two subsidiary principles state the same universality condition for, respectively, maxims of action and of ends.[18]

In separating these two principles falling immediately under the Categorical Imperative we take the first step in a description of the method for applying the Categorical Imperative. But before one can examine the details of the application of the supreme moral principle which Kant describes chiefly in the *Metaphysik der Sitten,* though also elsewhere, it is necessary to understand at a somewhat deeper level what it is for an agent to have a maxim. A complete account of Kant's theory of action would include an account of his theory of human willing and of human freedom, and so stray a long way from the main purpose of this examination of Kant's ethics. But some account of what it is for an agent to act on a principle or maxim is needed, even if the cost is a superficial treatment of Kant's theory of willing and of freedom.

Each of the phrases "acting on a maxim" and "acting on a principle" suggests that the agent must hold that principle or maxim for a considerable time; that his act must express a settled policy. This in turn suggests that many acts have no maxim, if the acts are done either on whim or without any commitment to act in the same way on other occasions. It would follow that some acts could not be morally assessed by examining the universality or otherwise of their maxims. But none of these propositions follows from Kant's ethical theory.

[16] *M.S.,* p. 231. Quoted from Ladd's translation, but putting "power of choice" for *Willkür* for the sake of consistency with quotations from Gregor's translations.

[17] *M.S.,* p. 394.

[18] Formula I is not the only formula of the Categorical Imperative to embrace two subsidiary formulas. For instance, the Formula of the End in Itself forbids treating men as mere means, and requires that we treat them as ends, *G.,* p. 429. One reason why the latter formula may seem more satisfactory if one concentrates on the *Grundlegung* is that Kant does not give two versions of Formula I there, although he clearly indicates that there are two ways in which the formula is to be applied when he distinguishes between the tests for wide and for narrow duty, *G.,* p. 424.

A maxim is a principle which, in Kant's terminology, expresses a determination of the power of choice.[19] To say that an agent's power of choice is determined is simply to say that he intends to do a specific sort of act or pursue a specific end in some situation. If an agent has a maxim "To do A if B," then he intends to do A if B.

Intentions, and so maxims, may or may not be formulated by the agent either on the occasion of acting or beforehand. Intentions may be intentions to do acts of some sort on some future occasion or sort of occasion (formulable in maxims of action) or they may be more general intentions to pursue certain sorts of ends (formulable in maxims of ends). If an agent has an intention to do or omit some act on a particular occasion or on occasions of particular sorts, then he may be said to have made a decision. If he intends to pursue a particular purpose in a variety of situations, then he may be said to have adopted a policy. Both decisions and policies may therefore be made or adopted by agents for use in recurrent situations. However, neither maxims of action nor maxims of ends *need* be retained for any length of time. While obvious for the case of maxims of action, this is also true for maxims of ends. A man might intend to do whatever was needed to develop some talent, but alter his policy as soon as he discovered how arduous its execution was.

There are also intentional acts where the agent has neither made any prior or present decision nor adopted any policy. A man might, for instance, have an extra cup of coffee at breakfast without either having decided in advance or on the spot to do so, or having any policy which required him to do so. But his act may still be intentional under some description or another (though it need not be: he might drink the coffee compulsively or otherwise involuntarily). The intention of such acts can also be formulated in a maxim of action, though the agent need not in this case formulate this maxim, even to the degree that he must formulate the maxims expressing his decisions

[19] Cf. *M.S.*, pp. 212–25. "Power of choice" or "choice" is Gregor's translation for *Willkür*, while she reserves "will" for *Wille*. Ladd translates *Willkür* by "will" (uncapitalized) and *Wille* by "Will." In earlier works, Kant does not distinguish *Willkür* from *Wille*, and speaks of maxims as expressing a determination of the "will" (*Wille*). Cf. e.g. *K.P.V.*, pp. 18–19. But since he also identified *Wille* with practical reason and held that practical reason could determine the will, this led to considerable confusion. Once *Wille* and *Willkür* are distinguished these matters sort themselves out. *Willkür* may be determined by practical reason, i.e. by *Wille* (in this case the agent's maxim conforms to the moral law); or it may be determined by ends desired and hypothetical imperatives (in which case the agent's maxim is a mere maxim).

and policies. He may say to himself "I feel a bit chilly this morning, so I'll have another cup to get warm." But he may not. Even so, his intention in acting could in principle be discovered—for instance, by finding out what changes in circumstances (if any) would have led him to decline the extra cup. His intention in acting could be stated in a maxim of action which could be ascribed to the agent.

Kant's solution to the problem of relevant descriptions is to claim that any voluntary act has a maxim to which the Categorical Imperative should be applied. This solution is adequate only if there is indeed a one–many correlation between maxims and acts and if we have reasons for thinking that a maxim is the appropriate principle for moral assessment. But it seems that neither of these claims holds. First, acts may be intended under a variety of descriptions. A man may intentionally raise his gun, fire it, and kill an enemy. May one ascribe a maxim incorporating each description under which his act is intentional to him? Or is one and only one intentional composite act description, to which one maxim corresponds, relevant in such cases? Second, may not some of the maxims ascribed to agents incorporate false, idiosyncratic, or otherwise "inappropriate," descriptions of their acts and policies? In all such cases, it seems the problem of relevant descriptions would arise.

The first of these objections, if it holds up, destroys Kant's solution to the problem of relevant descriptions. Hence, there is an immediate temptation to revise his position and seek among the various descriptions under which an act may be intended one which has some sort of primacy. Various proposals of this sort have been made, for instance by Anscombe and D'Arcy, and some of them will be discussed in chapter 7. However, I believe it would be a mistake to take the objection just raised as a grounds for embracing such proposals.

We want to be able to assess *all* aspects and phases of what we do. Hence, none of the maxims on which an agent acts is irrelevant to assessing the moral status of his acts. In the above objection it appeared that intending an act under various descriptions destroyed the one–many correlation between maxims and acts because "raising a gun, firing it, and killing an enemy" was construed as a single act, while the corresponding maxims were construed as three separate maxims. But the criteria of individuation for acts and maxims do not demand this construction. We may break down acts into components and phases to each of which a relatively specific maxim corresponds, or compound acts into sequences to each of which a compound or an abstract maxim corresponds. It is one of the merits of Kant's solution of the problem of relevant descriptions that it does not preclude us from assessing morally either small but intended components of our actions such as firing a gun or large intended sequences of actions such as "committing murder" or "betraying the cause."

The second objection raised to Kant's solution to the problem of relevant descriptions is less general, but more serious. Agents do often intend their acts under inappropriate descriptions. Chapters 6 and 7 will discuss and try to dispel some of the difficulties to which Kant's ethical theory is brought by his solution to the problem of relevant descriptions. In the meantime, I shall assume that Kant provides at least a partial solution to the problem of relevant descriptions when he applies his universality test to agents' maxims.

CHAPTER FOUR

ETHICAL CATEGORIES

A formal criterion for the moral status of acts, such as the Categorical Imperative, must begin by establishing a criterion for the moral status of some sort of principle. Formal conditions cannot apply directly to entities having no linguistic structure. Kant hopes the Categorical Imperative can be used directly to isolate certain maxims of duty. Since, as he thinks, any act has a single maxim, it will then be possible to determine the moral status of acts, by seeing what their maxim's status is. His claim is ambitious:

Those who know what a formula means to a mathematician in determining what is to be done in solving a problem without letting him go astray will not regard a formula which will do this for all duties as something insignificant and unnecessary.[1]

The Categorical Imperative is to provide in the first place a decision procedure for maxims of duty, and as a second step a decision procedure for the moral status of acts. It is not merely to differentiate those maxims and acts which are morally acceptable from those which are not. It is a precision instrument to test whether an act is obligatory, forbidden, or permissible, and also whether it is morally worthy, morally unworthy, or lacking in moral worth.

To make these distinctions Kant develops two separate methods of applying the Categorical Imperative. The next chapter will be devoted to examining the details of each of these tests and their effectiveness. I shall first examine in greater detail just which moral distinctions Kant hopes to make, and how he thinks they are related to one another. The universality tests advanced by Hare and Singer were thought to characterize, respectively, moral

[1] *K.P.V.,* p. 8, n.

principles or judgments in general and acceptable principles of right. Kant is clearly far more ambitious.

Making a map of Kant's various types of duty can seem as tedious as charting polar ice. There are plenty of features but they don't seem to fit into any pattern. The distinctions are introduced casually, and not always consistently, at various points in his writings on ethics, though chiefly in the *Metaphysik der Sitten.* Consequently a thicket of controversy has grown up about Kant's basic ethical categories.[2] To tame this material into fairly brief, manageable form, I shall neglect most of the disputes, and concentrate largely on Kant's writings. Even so, this chapter is the most solidly exegetical in this book; the argument can be pursued without reading the textual detail by turning to the summary on page 57.

The main division of the *Metaphysik der Sitten* is between the discussion of *duties of justice* and that of *duties of virtue.* These families of duties form, respectively, the subject matter of the *Rechtslehre* and of the *Tugendlehre.* The definition of a duty of each of these sorts is complex, and I shall take them in order.

⚜ I *Duties of Justice*

All duties of justice are derived from one of the restricted versions of the Formula of Universal Law, the Universal Principle of Justice, which runs "act externally in such a way that the free use of your will is compatible with the freedom of everyone according to universal law." The exact method by which this derivation proceeds will be discussed in the next chapter; here I shall consider the main characteristics of duties of justice. Kant claims that all duties of justice must be *legal* duties; they must be *narrow* duties, and they must be *perfect* duties. Each of these claims needs interpretation.

The notion of a legal duty contrasts with that of an ethical duty. The legal/ethical distinction, though not used in the *Grundlegung,* is one of the clearer distinctions that Kant draws between duties and has great importance in the *Metaphysik der Sitten.* Legal duties are those which an agent might be brought to fulfill by some other person or persons. Ethical duties are those

---

[2] See, for instance, M. Gregor, *Laws of Freedom;* P. Eisenberg, "Basic Ethical Categories in Kant's *Tugendlehre," American Philosophical Quarterly,* Vol. 3., 1966; T. E. Hill, "Kant on Imperfect Duty and Supererogation," *Kant-Studien,* Vol. 62, 1971.

which an agent cannot in principle be compelled to fulfill by anybody else.[3] It is impossible to compel, cajole or manipulate others into doing their ethical duty. These duties are duties to pursue certain ends rather than to do certain acts. The ends which ethical duty requires men to pursue are *obligatory ends*. The ends which an agent may be pursuing when fulfilling his legal duties may be of any sort whatever; on the whole they will be ends which the agent desires. Keeping a contract is an example of a legal duty, and may be fulfilled by agents with various sorts of ends. Developing whatever skills and talents one can in order to be more able to do things is an ethical duty, since any agent who does so must have (at least in part) the obligatory end which Kant calls "developing his perfection."

Kant attributes motives to agents on the basis of the sort of ends they have. An agent whose end it is to do his duty or to achieve one of the obligatory ends of the *Metaphysik der Sitten* (the relationship between these two will be examined in chapters 5 and 6) is said to have a *pure motive*. One whose end is some object of desire is said to act from *inclination* or from an *empirical motive*. This attribution of motives, I have already claimed, is simply a projection from the type of end an agent has, not an independent psychological theory. But the alternative vocabulary helps illuminate the legal/ethical distinction.

Ethical duties can be carried out only from a pure motive. But legal duties, which require only specific acts, may be carried out from any of a variety of empirical motives: for instance, from fear of punishment or from hope of some reward. Ethical duties must be self-imposed; legal duties need not be. However, it is also possible to do any legal duty from a pure motive, which Kant calls *reverence for the law* or the *sense of duty*. All legal duties are *indirectly ethical*.[4] In Kant's terminology these contrasts between legal and ethical duties are summed up by saying that the former may be *externally legislated*, while the latter must be *internally legislated*.[5]

It is clear why any duty falling under the universal principle of justice must be a legal duty. Since that principle regulates *external* action, anything it requires might also be imposed by using external sanctions or incentives of one sort or another. Duties of justice must be externally legislatable, hence are legal duties.

The second feature of duties of justice to which Kant draws attention is that they must be *narrow* (strict or rigorous) duties as opposed to *wide* (broad)

[3] *M.S.*, p. 218.   [4] *M.S.*, p. 221.   [5] *M.S.*, p. 219.

duties.[6] This distinction has nothing to do with the legislation of duties, but it seems as though Kant thinks that the legal/ethical distinction coincides with the narrow/wide distinction. He writes: "Ethical duties are all of wide obligation, whereas juridical [legal] duties are of narrow obligation." [7]

Before accepting this claim it is necessary to find out on what basis duties are to be classified as "narrow" or "wide." Though the distinction is first introduced in the *Grundlegung,* it is not used in any argument there. The terms are simply applied to those duties established by the first and second methods respectively, of applying the Formula of Universal Law. In the *Metaphysik der Sitten* there is a far more detailed account of the distinction. Wide duties are duties to have certain ends; their wideness consists in the fact that often a variety of means to any ends is available to an agent, none of which is mandatory. In such cases an agent has some latitude in doing his duty. Narrow duties on the other hand are duties to do specific acts; here an agent has no latitude in doing his duty. Wide duties are expressed in maxims of ends; narrow duties in maxims of action. Wide duties are duties to have policies; narrow duties are duties to do certain acts (whether or not these acts implement prior decisions).

The argument to show that this distinction coincides with that between legal and ethical duties is simple. Legal duties must be narrow, i.e., must prescribe or proscribe acts, because others can exact from us only specific acts or omissions, and not the pursuit of any end. Ethical duties must be wide, i.e., must require the adoption of certain policies, because we cannot be compelled to adopt policies.

Although this argument is simple it is fallacious. Though ethical duties cannot be exacted from us by others, it does not follow that they must be duties to adopt policies. There may also be some acts which others cannot constrain us to do. Duties which can be externally legislated must all be duties to do or to refrain from acts; but it does not follow that all duties to do or refrain from acts must be externally legislated. Kant does not classify all duties to do or refrain from acts as duties of justice. Among duties of virtue he includes the duty to refrain from lying and self-deception. So at least some duties of virtue, all of which are supposed to be ethical duties, are duties to omit acts. Worse still, some duties of virtue require omissions that could be externally legislated, such as refraining from suicide or mockery. The initial identification of the distinction between narrow and wide duties and that between legal and ethical duties cannot be sustained.

[6] *G.,* p. 424; *M.S.,* pp. 389–90.   [7] *Ibid.*

Some of these difficulties can be resolved by untangling two senses in which Kant uses the narrow/wide distinction. In the phrase quoted above he speaks of duties as being narrow or wide *in obligation,* and draws a distinction between two ways of establishing a duty. There are *duties of narrow obligation* which are duties because certain acts or omissions can be shown obligatory; there are *duties of wide obligation* which are duties because certain ends can be shown obligatory. But he also distinguishes between duties of wide and of narrow *requirement. Duties of narrow requirement* are fulfilled by specific acts and omissions; *duties of wide requirement* by adopting and implementing certain policies. The requirement that duties impose need not be of the same sort as their obligation. Certain duties of wide obligation may require specific acts and omissions as means to obligatory ends. The duties to refrain from mockery, self-deceit, suicide, or drunkenness fall in this category.[8]

When we refer to the sort of obligation a duty has, we indicate the type of derivation that can be given to justify the duty. A duty of narrow obligation is justified by applying the Formula of Universal Law to an agent's maxim of action, i.e., by applying the Universal Principle of Justice. A duty of wide obligation is justified by applying the formula to the agent's maxim of ends, i.e., by applying the first principle of the doctrine of virtue. When we refer to the sort of requirement a duty imposes we indicate how it is to be fulfilled. A duty of narrow requirement points to a specific act or omission as obligatory.[9] A duty of wide requirement does not. It points to a policy

[8] P. Eisenberg, p. 262, including note, suggests that there are not two distinctions, but rather "one continuum of duties that are of wider and narrower obligation." This interpretation certainly fits Kant's confusing classification of perfect duties to oneself and duties of respect both as wide and as narrow. But it does not help us to understand the basis for this classification, which lies in the fact that Kant is making two closely related distinctions which do not coincide.

[9] Kant is quite aware that there can be a great deal of variation in the precision with which maxims of action determine a duty of narrow requirement. We have often some choice over how we fulfill a duty of justice. For instance, we may pay some debts in cash, by check, or in kind. This point has been argued, for instance, by R. Chisholm, "Supererogation and Offence", *Ratio,* 5 (1963), 4n., as an objection to any distinction between duties which allow latitude and those which do not. But this argument only shows that judgment is needed in applying any principle, that principles cannot be fully specific. It does not show that the duty to pay our debts is a duty of wide requirement. The degree of freedom we have in acting on a maxim of action is quite different from the degree of freedom we have in pursuing a certain end. In a sense, inclination has the greater liberty in the former case. It is arbitrary, from the point of view of justice, which method of payment is chosen. But in pursuing a certain end the choice between alternative acts is not always arbitrary, rather it depends on their estimated effectiveness as means to the ends.

which must be adopted. Of course, adoption of a policy requires specific acts and omissions, but what these are to be may vary from context to context. Fulfilling duties of wide requirement is not a passive matter, but duty does not determine just which acts or omissions are needed.

All duties of justice must be duties of narrow obligation. This follows from the definition of the two phrases: each is applied to a duty in virtue of its being justified by appeal to the Universal Principle of Justice. Less obviously, but also clearly, all duties of justice must be narrow in their requirement. Any duty justified by applying the Formula of Universal Law to a maxim of action must be a duty to do or omit a specific act.

The third condition that Kant lays on duties of justice and on some of the duties of virtue which make narrow requirements is that they must be *perfect* duties.[10] Kant's commentators seem agreed that the distinction between perfect and imperfect duties is very important—yet also that Kant used these terms to mark different distinctions at different times. I shall argue that though these terms were traditionally used to mark an important distinction of philosophical ethics, Kant places little weight on the distinction. This is suggested by the following facts.

In the early *Vorlesung* the terms "perfect" and "imperfect" are used to indicate the sorts of duty which Kant later calls, respectively, legal and ethical. They mark a distinction between the ways in which duties can be legislated. In the *Grundlegung* [11] Kant defines perfect duties as those in whose execution no exception in the interests of inclination is permitted. This basis for distinguishing perfect from imperfect duties is again mentioned in the first part of the *Metaphysik der Sitten,* the *Rechtslehre.*[12] This definition suggests, and indeed encourages, an identification of the perfect/imperfect distinction with the narrow/wide distinction, which Paton makes both in his translation of the *Grundlegung* [13] and in his commentary [14] on it, which Gregor assumes in her commentary on the *Tugendlehre,*[15] and which Eisenberg accepts in his recent attempt to clarify the perfect/imperfect distinction.[16]

Since I have now distinguished two senses of the narrow/wide distinction, this claim needs to be re-examined. Perfect duties clearly cannot consist only

[10] *G.,* p. 421; *M.S.,* p. 389.   [11] *G.,* p. 422n.   [12] *M.S.,* p. 233.
[13] H. J. Paton, *The Moral Law,* p. 139.
[14] H. J. Paton, *The Categorical Imperative,* p. 148.   [15] M. Gregor, p. 97.
[16] P. Eisenberg, p. 257n.

of duties of narrow obligation, for then they would all be duties of justice. But Kant lists a large number of "perfect duties to oneself" in the *Tugend-lehre,* which is concerned only with duties of wide obligation. Are perfect duties then duties of narrow requirement? This identification seems much more plausible, since Kant's examples of "perfect duties to oneself" are all duties to do or omit specific acts or patterns of action. But though the per-fect/imperfect distinction may *coincide* with that between duties of narrow and of wide requirement, there is no sufficient reason for holding that the two distinctions are *identical.*

The latitude which imperfect duties are said to have in the *Grundlegung* (permitting exceptions) does not seem to belong to any duties according to the *Metaphysik der Sitten.*[17] And certainly the sort of latitude which duties of wide requirement allow—that of choosing among alternative ways to realize an obligatory end—is quite different. We are faced with the following dilemma: If we assume, contrary to the textual evidence, that the latitude of imperfect duties is that of duties of wide requirement, so that the two dis-tinctions are identical, then we can drop the perfect/imperfect distinction, since all Kant's arguments and the majority of his exposition are conducted in terms of the distinction between duties to pursue ends and duties to do specific acts, i.e., the distinction between duties of wide and of narrow requirement.[18] If, on the other hand, we assume that the two distinctions are not the same, then we do not know the basis for the perfect/imperfect distinction in the *Metaphysik der Sitten,* nor can we link it up with any of the other distinctions which Kant makes in that work. The alleged importance of the perfect/imperfect distinction was contingent on its identification with the narrow/wide requirement distinction. Since that identification cannot be sustained, I shall assume that the doctrine of the *Metaphysik der Sitten* can be discussed successfully without any further investigation of the perfect/imper-fect distinction.

Duties of justice can, therefore, be sufficiently characterized as narrow in obligation (i.e., justified by the Universal Principle of Justice), narrow in requirement, and legal in their legislation. The first of these conditions is the most general, and the other two depend on it. In the next chapter I want

[17] *M.S.,* p. 389, and P. Eisenberg, pp. 264–65.

[18] We might keep the "perfect"/"imperfect" *terminology* as a substitute for the dis-tinction between duties of wide and of narrow requirement. I do not favor this since the use of the term "imperfect" is linked in *G.* to the permitting of exceptions, which can mislead. But cf. T. E. Hill, pp. 55–67, for another view on this.

to show how a maxim of action should be tested to determine whether it is a maxim of justice. But here I shall only list the moral statuses Kant assigns to acts and omissions required or forbidden by maxims of justice.

Duties of justice, being legal duties, determine the *legal status* (or we might say, more fashionably, the *deontic status*) of acts. They require agents in appropriate circumstances to perform or refrain from certain acts. When they do so, their act or omission *conforms to* or *accords with* duty.[19] Such acts and omissions have *legality;* they are *right, just,* or *morally correct;* to do them is to do what is *due, owed,* or *obligatory.*[20] Acts and omissions which violate duties of justice are *wrong, unjust, forbidden,* or *impermissible.* Acts and omissions neither conforming to nor violating any duty of justice are *merely permissible.*[21]

Duties of justice are also indirectly ethical duties. Hence, acts fulfilling or violating them have an ethical status as well as a legal status. When a duty of justice is carried out as an ethical duty the agent's end is to do his duty. He acts from a pure and not from an empirical motive. Such principled action not merely accords with duty but is also said to be done *from duty* or *for the sake of duty;* it does not merely have legality, but also has *morality, moral value,* or *moral worth.*[22] To do one's legal duty from a pure motive is to do what is *virtuous* or *meritorious;* to carry it out, not in this way, but incidentally on some other maxim of ends, is not vicious but merely *lacking in moral worth,* as is any performance of forbidden or merely permissible acts.[23]

In the *Grundlegung,* Kant speaks as though it were always possible to act in accordance with duty without acting for the sake of duty. But, in fact, it is only duties to do particular acts (mainly duties of justice) which can be

---

[19] *G.,* p. 406.

[20] *K.P.V.,* p. 159; *M.S.,* pp. 214, 221–24, 226, 233–34, 389.

[21] *M.S.,* p. 221, *G.,* p. 439.   [22] *G.,* p. 406; *M.S.,* p. 224.

[23] For present purposes, no distinction need be drawn between any of the triads virtuous/lacking in virtue/vicious, meritorious/lacking in merit/demeritorious (the latter term is not used in the adjectival form), and morally worthy/lacking in moral worth/morally unworthy. The first member of each triad can be applied indifferently to acts and omissions which fulfill a duty of justice for the sake of duty and acts which aim at some obligatory end. (This contrast, we shall see in chapter 6, is only superficial.) Kant, in fact, uses the term "virtuous" only derivatively of acts and primarily of the sort of will which produces such acts. Virtue is "moral strength of will," *M.S.,* p. 404; virtuous acts are those which require such moral strength. For clarity I shall usually use the terminology of moral worth.

fulfilled in either of these two ways. For a duty of wide requirement—i.e., a duty to adopt a particular obligatory end—is not a duty to do a particular set of acts, which might be done from some empirical motive. The acts and omissions required by such duties are indeterminate, apart from a specific empirical context.

Duties of justice are then principles by which we can decide whether certain acts or omissions are obligatory, forbidden, or merely permissible. But it cannot be said that Kant's account of justice, i.e., his *Rechtslehre*, provides a complete theory of right action. The duties with which it deals are only a part of those which we (and Kant) regard as having to do with rightness and wrongness. There is no place in a theory of justice for assessing conduct beyond the scope of possible legislation, for the assessment of acts which, even if universally done, would not violate others' freedom. A theory of justice cannot consider wrongs we might do ourselves, or acts which, though they wrong others, cannot be legislated against.

II Duties of Virtue

It was possible to discuss the principal features of duties of justice without going into the various subdivisions into which Kant classifies these duties. It is far harder to understand what a duty of virtue is, in part because Kant groups such a heterogeneous collection of duties under this heading. A reasonable way to begin understanding them is to look at the organization of the *Tugendlehre*. This may be represented, with some simplifications, in Table 4.1.

Table 4.1

Duties of Virtue

Duties to Ourselves		Duties to Others	
Duties of omission (perfect duties to oneself: as an animal and as a moral being)	Duties of commission (imperfect duties to oneself: as an animal and as a moral being)	Duties of omission (duties of respect)	Duties of commission (duties of love)

If we assume that the narrow/wide distinction is unequivocally a distinction between duties to adopt policies and duties to do acts—i.e., is only a distinction between the requirements of duties—this organization is baffling, for all duties of virtue are said to be wide. Yet of the classes of duties listed only the two sorts of ethical duty of commission require the adoption of ends rather than specific acts and omissions. Among the perfect duties to oneself are prohibitions on suicide, drunkenness, self-abuse, and gluttony, as well as on various sorts of dishonesty. Among the duties of respect to others are prohibitions on mockery and detraction.

If we recognize that these duties, though wide in obligation, are narrow in requirement, the apparent inconsistencies can be resolved. If we do not distinguish wideness of obligation from wideness of requirement, they are multiplied. Then we are left with a large number of duties which are said to be wide but which are duties to do or to omit certain acts or patterns of action; which meet neither the conditions for being a duty of justice (since they could be universally violated without infringing another's freedom) nor those for being a duty of virtue (since they do not require the adoption of ends).

An interpretation of the *Metaphysik der Sitten* which makes no distinction between wideness of obligation and of requirement would have to deal with these anomalies. It is instructive to see where one such attempt leads. Gregor, in *Laws of Freedom,* concludes, for the reasons just given, that the division of duties into those of justice and those of virtue cannot be exhaustive. Her problem is to explain what the anomalous duties are like and how they are to be derived. She claims that the perfect duties to oneself are part of "moral philosophy in general," [24] in that they are ethical but narrow duties. They are derived neither from the Universal Principle of Justice nor from the first principle of the doctrine of virtue, but directly from the undifferentiated Categorical Imperative.[25]

If this interpretation is correct, there must be a special category of duties consisting of perfect duties to oneself as a moral being. But this does not solve the whole problem. Perfect duties to oneself as an animal being and duties of respect to others also require acts or omissions, not the adoption of policies. None of these duties is of wide requirement, and they could be fulfilled without internal legislation, contrary to Gregor's claim.[26] So her in-

[24] M. Gregor, p. 116.   [25] *Ibid.,* p. 117.

[26] Kant, too, appears to overlook this in calling both "perfect duties to oneself as an animal being" and duties of respect to others *ethical* duties of omission. These du-

terpretation yields only a partial explanation for the heterogeneity of Kant's list of duties of virtue. It also leads her to insist that there must be a narrower, technical sense of "duty of virtue" which includes only duties to adopt ends, and a wider sense which covers all ethical duties,[27] perfect duties to oneself being duties of virtue only in the looser sense. This contention is hard to reconcile with the text of the *Metaphysik der Sitten,* and Gregor has to conclude her chapter on perfect duties by allowing that they are something of an anomaly.

Distinguishing two senses of the narrow/wide distinction is a far more plausible way of resolving the textual difficulties of the *Metaphysik der Sitten* than any distinction between two senses of 'duty of virtue'. First, it enables one to understand Kant's classification of all "ethical duties of omission," and not just his treatment of perfect duties to onself as a moral being. All these duties are duties to omit certain acts or patterns of action, and so are narrow in requirement. That they are narrow in one sense Kant indicates by calling all these duties "limiting" or "negative" and even "narrow," contrasting this with ethical duties of commission which are "widening" or "positive" as well as "wide." [28] But both sorts of duty are always classified as duties of virtue; they both duties of wide obligation since they all fall under one or another obligatory end and can only be shown to be duties by applying the first principle of the doctrine of virtue. There is no basis for thinking that there are any duties belonging to moral philosophy in general which are neither duties of justice nor duties of virtue. "Ethical duties of omission" though narrow in requirement meet sufficient conditions for being duties of virtue: they can be derived only by applying the Formula of Universal Law to maxims of ends, i.e., from the first principle of the doctrine of virtue.

Duties of virtue can be characterized in general terms. All these duties are wide in obligation because they fall under some obligatory end. Kant thinks

---

ties, in fact, require omissions which could be externally legislated. Refraining from suicide, drunkenness, self-abuse, mockery, detraction, and so on could be exacted from us by others. This is not so for those omissions which are required by perfect duties to oneself as a moral being—refraining from lying, self-deception, and so on. These do need internal legislation. Those ethical duties of omission which can be externally legislated can, like duties of justice, also be internally legislated. But they are not the same as duties of justice since they are always of wide obligation. Odd as it may sound, they are legal duties of virtue.

[27] M. Gregor, pp. 119–22.   [28] *M.S.,* pp. 418, 449.

that there are two such ends: one's own perfection and the happiness of others, to which all other duties of virtue are subordinate. The derivation of these obligatory ends will be taken up in the next chapter. Particular duties of virtue may be related in either of two ways to these obligatory ends. They may require that some indispensable means to these ends be taken, or that some subsidiary policy to achieve a part of the obligatory end be adopted. To refrain from suicide is to ensure that a necessary means to one's own perfection is implemented; to do what may be needed to help others in need is to pursue a policy which is part of the policy of promoting others' happiness.

The distinction between the obligation and the requirement of duties does not solve all the problems of the *Tugendlehre*. For that distinction does not explain why Kant should claim that all the narrow requirements of duties of virtue should be duties to refrain from acts. And an inspection of Kant's list of "ethical duties of omission" suggests that some of these narrow requirements require acts rather than omissions. Respect for others and refraining from suicide may require more than omissions from us. But even if the "ethical duties of omission" are misnamed, their classification is clear. "Ethical duties of omission" cannot be shown duties except by showing that some end is obligatory, and then that these acts or omissions are indispensable means to that end. They are duties of virtue. But though wide in obligation, they are narrow in requirement. What they demand could be enjoined in a maxim of action rather than in a maxim of ends. Some of these wide duties of narrow requirement actually demand acts and omissions which could be externally legislated; but most of them always need internal legislation, and all of them need it when done as part of a policy of pursuing an obligatory end.

The similarity between "ethical duties of omission" and duties of justice suggests that the former too may be fulfilled or violated in either of two ways. They may be fulfilled as duties when the agent is in fact pursuing the appropriate obligatory end, or they may be fulfilled incidentally in the course of the agent's pursuit of some other end. They may be violated intentionally when the agent intends to prevent the realization of some obligatory end, or they may be violated incidentally in the course of pursuing some other end.

This intuition is borne out by the fact that Kant assigns to acts which fulfill and violate ethical duties of omission different combinations of moral statuses from those which he assigns to acts which fulfill and violate ethical duties of commission. Acts fulfilling ethical duties of omission are *right* in the sense of *obligatory;* for since these acts are nonoptional means to obligatory ends they cannot be merely permissible, let alone forbidden. Kant's theory of right is more extensive than his theory of justice. If such acts are principled, i.e., done on a maxim of achieving that end, they are also *meritorious* or *morally worthy;* if done incidentally, i.e., on any other maxim of ends, they *lack moral worth.* Acts violating ethical duties of omission are *wrong;* if the violation is principled (done on a maxim of not pursuing an obligatory end), it is *vicious.* If it occurs incidentally in the pursuit of some other end, the situation is not so clearcut. On the basis of the *Grundlegung,* one might expect such acts to be merely lacking in moral worth. But in the *Metaphysik der Sitten,* Kant usually classifies all violations of ethical duties of omission as vicious.[29]

Acts and omissions fulfilling ethical duties of commission must all be done on a maxim of pursuing an obligatory end. Of course, the agent must also have a maxim of action, determined by his choice of a means to that end. Determining whether an act fulfills an ethical duty of commission is a two-stage affair. The agent must have an obligatory end and he must be acting in a way which will realize that end. Either of these stages can go wrong. So there are two ways in which it is possible to violate an ethical duty of commission. An agent may have a maxim of ends which is incompatible with some obligatory end. He may, for instance, intend not to promote others' happiness. Or he may have an obligatory end, but, whether through ignorance or from slackness, slip up in implementing that end. (Such slip-ups cannot be total: a man who never does anything likely to achieve the obligatory end which he claims to hold simply provides excellent evidence that his claim is unjustified, not excellent evidence of peculiarly frequent slip-ups). When the agent has a maxim of ends that is incompatible with an obligatory end, his policy is vicious, and so are the acts he does to implement it. When his aim is an obligatory end and his failure to implement it due to some slackness or laxity, his violations of duty simply lack moral worth; they are what Kant calls *peccata.* Fulfillments of ethical duties of omission lack moral worth, unless they are part of a virtuous policy; violations of ethical duties of commission merely lack moral worth, unless they are part of a vicious policy. But violations of ethical duties of commission that lack moral worth are not incidental violations of the duty, in the sense

---

[29] See *M.S.,* p. 463, for an explicit statement for the case of duties of respect; see usage throughout *M.S.,* pp. 421–44, for perfect duties to oneself.

in which there can be incidental violations and fulfillments of ethical duties of omission (and, for that matter, of duties of justice). They are not violations dependent on the pursuit of a nonobligatory end. Since ethical duties of commission are indeterminate in their requirements, one cannot speak of acts as violating and fulfilling them in abstraction from agents' maxims of ends. The violations of ethical duties of commission which lack moral worth are acts done by agents who fail to take appropriate means to their (obligatory) end.

These classifications of the legal and moral statuses of acts may be summarized in a table, using O for "obligatory," P for "merely permissible," F for "forbidden," m for "morally worthy" ("meritorious" or "virtuous"), lm for "lacking in moral worth," and v for "vicious" (or "morally unworthy").

Table 4.2

	Fulfillments		Violations		
	Inci-dental	Prin-cipled	Inci-dental	Prin-cipled	Violation due to slackness, despite obligatory end
Duties of justice	$O; lm$	$O; m$	$F; lm$	$F; lm$	
Ethical duties of omission	$O; lm$	$O; m$	$F; v(?)$	$F; v$	
Ethical duties of commission	not defined	m	not defined	v	lm

No legal status has been assigned to acts fulfilling and violating ethical duties of commission. They do, of course, have such a status, but it depends wholly on the maxim of action concerned. And since this is not determined except for specific contexts by the obligatory maxim of ends (as is the case with ethical duties of omission), nothing general can be said about the legal status of such acts. Kant tends to think such acts will be merely permissible.

All acts falling outside the categories of the above table would be merely permissible and without moral worth.

III Conclusions

Kant's division of human duties into duties of justice and duties of virtue is a division between two ways of showing what is morally required. Duties of justice are duties because of the sort of acts they enjoin; duties of virtue are duties because of the sort of ends they require us to pursue. In Kant's terminology, duties of justice are of narrow obligation; duties of virtue of wide obligation.

Like many writers Kant does not think that a theory of justice is the whole of a theory of right action. The obligatory ends which duties of virtue require us to pursue demand certain specifiable acts and omissions. These nonoptional means to obligatory ends are the controversial 'ethical duties of omission.' These duties are of narrow requirement, i.e., they demand acts or omissions even though they are of wide obligation. The other duties of virtue are wide in requirement as well as in obligation: no general rules can specify the acts and omissions that may be required in their pursuit. Kant thinks that the duties of virtue which make narrow requirements will all be duties to abstain from certain acts. But this is presumably due to empirical considerations about the indispensable means to obligatory ends.

All duties of justice can be imposed on us by others: they are externally legislatable. However, only some of the ethical duties of omission (e.g.,

Table 4.3

Duties of narrow obligation	Duties of wide obligation		
Duties of Justice	Duties of Virtue		
/////////	Ethical duties of omission		Ethical duties of commission
/////////	Duties to do/omit outer acts	Duties to do/omit inner acts	

Duties of narrow requirement — Duties of wide requirement

The duties in the shaded area are ones which others can impose.

refraining from mockery) could be imposed upon us from without. Others cannot require us to perform ethical duties of omission such as refraining from self-deception. The ethical duties of commission, being all duties to pursue ends, cannot be imposed by others.

The relationships between duties of different sorts can be shown clearly in Table 4.3.

CHAPTER FIVE

APPLYING THE CATEGORICAL IMPERATIVE

The complex classification of duties and of the moral statuses of acts in chapter 4 shows that the Categorical Imperative must have great powers of discrimination if it is really to provide a method for solving all those ethical problems for which Kant thinks it is appropriate. To most recent commentators, and to many earlier ones, it has seemed quite clear that the Categorical Imperative cannot be used to solve ethical problems. Mill wrote of Kant:

But when he begins to deduce from this precept any of the actual duties of morality, he fails, almost grotesquely, to show that there would be any contradiction, any logical (not to say physical) impossibility in the adoption by all rational beings of the most outrageously immoral rules of conduct.[1]

And a recent commentator, T. C. Williams, remarks:

The traditional . . . view of . . . the categorical imperative . . . as offering a precise standard or criterion against which the moral value of proposed actions might be tested . . . is unrewarding, for the strain in Kant's thought which is emphasized by these writers and taken as representative of his basic position leads to a number of bizarre conclusions . . . which, perforce, have been universally rejected by commentators.[2]

It is certainly true that views both grotesque and bizarre have been attributed to Kant in the course of various discussions of the application of the Categorical Imperative. To use the Formula of Universal Law as a test of the moral status of acts is often held to commit one to rigorism—to the view that all moral principles must be very general. Sometimes it is thought to involve the claim that all acts must be either obligatory or forbidden, and

---

[1] J. S. Mill, *Utilitarianism*, p. 4.　　[2] T. C. Williams, pp. 37–8.

that there is no other moral status or that principles of action can be logically deduced from a purely formal principle, or that moral principles must abstract from ends, and even that any act which is enjoyed must be immoral. The inadequacies of these attributions have been well documented, particularly by Ebbinghaus and Paton, and more recently by Singer and Williams.[3] It would, therefore, not be fruitful to go over past commentaries to see whether each is just or not in its attribution of grotesque and bizarre viewpoints.

However, there is also no need to retreat and conclude, as some recent writers have done, that the Categorical Imperative cannot give any detailed practical guidance, but must be no more than a descriptive principle which "describes the working of pure practical reason," or at best is a principle "which is able to lead to an understanding of the nature of moral action." [4] It is possible that the commentaries are at fault and that the Categorical Imperative can give detailed practical guidance. Here I shall try to give an interpretation of the method for applying the Categorical Imperative which meets three standards. First, it will be a plausible reading of the Kantian texts; second, it will be able to classify the moral status of (at any rate most) acts, i.e., it will make the distinctions which Kant claims it can make; third, it will assign acts to these categories in a way which, by and large, confirms our intuition.

A good place to begin this enterprise is with the passage in which Kant first sketches his two procedures for applying the Formula of Universal Law.

In the *Grundlegung* Kant writes:

We must *be able to will* that a maxim of our action should become a universal law—this is the general canon for all moral judgment of an action. Some actions are so constituted that their maxim cannot even be *conceived* as a universal law of a nature without a contradiction, let alone *willed* as what *ought* to become one. In the case of others we do not find this inner impossibility, but it is still impossible to *will* that

---

[3] For examples of the sorts of bizarre interpretations instanced cf. e.g., A. C. Ewing, especially p. 43; C. D. Broad, *Five Types of Ethical Theory*, ch. 5, especially pp. 119, 120, 124, 127–28; S. Körner, *Kant*, p. 135. See also the references to such interpretations given in the various works of rebuttal: J. Ebbinghaus, "Interpretation and Misinterpretation of the Categorical Imperative," *Philosophical Quarterly*, Vol. 4, 1954; H. J. Paton, *The Categorical Imperative;* M. Singer, chs. 8, 9, pp. 217–99; T. C. Williams, ch. 4, pp. 37–56.

[4] Notably A. R. C. Duncan, *Practical Reason and Morality*, cf. especially p. 71, and T. C. Williams, cf. especially ch. 9, pp. 116–32.

their maxim should be raised to the universality of a law of nature, because such a will would contradict itself. It is easily seen that the first kind of action is opposed to strict or narrow (rigorous) duty, the second only to wider (meritorious) duty . . .[5]

The sense in which these two tests discriminate wide from narrow duty (if they are indeed able to do so) must be that they discriminate between maxims of wide and narrow obligation. No test is needed to discriminate between maxims of wide and narrow requirement, since this is given by the form of the maxim, maxims of ends being all of wide requirement and maxims of action all of narrow requirement. But if this test discriminates maxims of wide obligation from those of narrow obligation, then it also discriminates maxims of virtue from maxims of justice, for the two distinctions coincide. So the division of this chapter into a section called "Contradiction in Conception" and another called "Contradiction in the Will" will correspond to the division of the previous chapter into a section called "Duties of Justice" and one called "Duties of Virtue." But before proceeding to either of these sections I shall lay out the argument pattern shared by both types of application of Formula I of the Categorical Imperative.

If we are to decide whether we can will the maxim of our action as a universal law, a plausible initial step is to take the maxim and state it in universalized form. Suppose the maxim can be rendered schematically:

(3) To − − − − if · · · ·

The universalized counterpart of (3) would be

(5) Everybody to − − − − if · · · ·

A universalized maxim is, however, still a practical principle, not a universal law of nature, and Kant raises the problem that

. . . since all instances of possible actions are only empirical, it seems absurd to wish to find a case in the world of sense, and thus standing under a law of nature, which admits the application of a law of freedom to it.[6]

How then can we judge whether acts fall under a particular universalized maxim, or when the universalized maxim can be willed as a law of nature?

[5] *G.*, p. 424.   [6] *K.P.V.*, p. 68.

Kant intends to obviate this difficulty by considering the possibility of acts falling not under the universalized maxim, i.e., the practical principle, but under an analogous natural law which he calls the *type* of the (putative) moral law.[7]

The typified practical principle which we consider for this purpose can be rendered schematically by:

(6) Everybody will − − − − if . . . .

A formula of this form which corresponds to a given maxim of form (3) or (3′) will be called the *universalized typified counterpart* (for short: *UTC*) of that maxim.

The relationship between a particular practical principle and its type is the clue to the relationship between the Formula of Universal Law and the Formula of the Law of Nature. The latter formula specifies more precisely than the former what must be done when we 'will a maxim as universal law' if the result of this operation is to guide our actions. In the *Critique of Practical Reason*, Kant spells out in more detail just what the role of Formula Ia of the Categorical Imperative is:

The rule of judgment under laws of pure practical reason is: ask youself whether, if the action you propose should take place by a law of nature of which you yourself were a part, you could regard it as possible through your own will.[8]

There is no question here of whether the act taking place would be regarded as desirable, but only whether it can be regarded as possible. By the device of considering a fictitious law of nature we are supposed to be able to decide whether the maxim of an act can pass the test of being willed as a law of nature.

Another way of spelling out the reason for considering, not universalized maxims that can be stated schematically in form (5), but their typified coun-

---

[7] *K.P.V.*, p. 70. Kant sometimes, and with misgivings, calls the type of a moral law the schema of the law. This terminology will be avoided (a) because Kant himself agrees that the analogy with schemata which enable us to exhibit objects falling under concepts of nature is misleading, and (b) because the term "schema" is here being used to refer to various more or less abstract ways of stating maxims.

[8] *K.P.V.*, p. 69.

terparts of form (6) when testing whether maxims are maxims of duty, is this. A universalized maxim is not a statement. Hence, the question of whether it contains a contradiction does not arise. Only if the composite act description of the original maxim was incoherent would it make sense to speak of a universalized maxim as containing a contradiction. But Kant would not, I think, have considered anything of the form "to — — — — if · · · ·" a maxim if the element "— — — — if · · · ·" were not coherent.[9] He therefore rules out this sense in which maxims could be said to contain a contradiction.

The concepts which can be applied appropriately to practical principles, such as universalized maxims, are those of being "self-defeating" or "self-frustrating." But if the criteria for applying the concept of a contradiction are clearer than those for determining self-defeat or self-frustration, then it may be desirable to test maxims by considering their UTC's. There the sort of maxim which Kant wants to show incompatible with duty will be represented by a law of nature which contains a contradiction. Kant does not want to depend on relatively opaque concepts like those of being self-defeating or self-frustrating in his test of which maxims cannot be practical laws. Rather he wants to provide a method for mapping instances of such concepts onto the much more readily identifiable instances of the concept of a contradiction.

I Contradiction in Conception

We have now to see how the UTC's of maxims contrary to duty generate contradictions. To do this the two tests Kant proposes must be considered separately. The contradiction in conception test has usually been thought reasonably clear but extremely weak, though it has also received its share of bizarre interpretations, which I shall not review. However, I shall take the time to show that the most plausible interpretations proposed for this test are also unconvincing. This is partly because they turn out to be very weak, while Kant clearly thought that the contradiction in conception test had considerable power, and partly because they cannot be supported by the text. An alternative interpretation shows that the test is able to do a

[9] In effect, Kant is assuming that agents intend to do only coherent acts. This is not a trivial assumption, see chapter 6, sections IV and V.

great deal that Kant expects it to do and also receives considerable textual support.

Paton, followed by Beck,[10] thinks that a complete explanation of the use of the UTC of a practical principle requires us to take into consideration that Kant thinks laws of nature are teleological and collectively characterize a harmonious natural order, and that this explains

how Kant can pass, without any statement of his ground, from the formal law of nature to teleological laws of human nature as a basis for the rightness and wrongness of our maxims. He is justified in doing this, as I have suggested, because he is dealing with human maxims and human character, which must be regarded as purposive.[11]

This amounts to interpreting the type of the moral law as more than an heuristic device by which a contradiction (either in conception or in the will—Paton does not make much of the difference between the two tests) [12] may be more explicitly exhibited. It amounts to seeing any application of Formula I of the Categorical Imperative as interpretable only in the light of the *Formula of the Kingdom of Ends*, which reads "So act as if you were always through your maxims a law-making member of the kingdom of ends." [13] The harmonious natural order would typify a kingdom of ends.

Certainly Kant does think that human maxims are purposive. Also, he thinks that maxims of duty would form collectively an intelligible moral order, and for this order he thinks that the harmonious natural order can serve as a type or model. But I cannot find in Kant's discussion of the type of the moral law any support for the contention that Kant is primarily concerned with typifying the moral order by the natural order rather than typifying particular (putative) moral laws by particular (hypothetical) natural laws. If he were more concerned with the former task, then the type of a particular maxim would hardly help us to clarify that maxim's status. We would have to decide whether an action done on the maxim was one of those "whose maxims, if conceived as a law of nature, would further a systematic harmony of purposes among men, or at least would do nothing to destroy such a systematic harmony." [14]

This suggests that we could not test the status of maxims individually,

[10] H. J. Paton, *The Categorical Imperative*, pp. 157–64; L. W. Beck, *A Commentary on Kant's Critique of Practical Reason*, pp. 157–63.

[11] H. J. Paton, *The Categorical Imperative*, p. 162.   [12] *Ibid.*, p. 157.

[13] *G.*, p. 438.   [14] H. J. Paton, *The Categorical Imperative*, p. 163.

but only the status of proposed systems of maxims, an implausibly difficult task. Yet Kant emphasizes the practical value of considering possible natural laws which we treat as types for particular maxims. Further, if purposiveness is to be introduced into every explanation of the role of typifying practical principles, then we may be at a loss to see what differentiates maxims that cannot be conceived as universal laws of nature (and so cannot be maxims of justice) from maxims that merely cannot be willed as universal laws of nature (and so cannot be maxims of any sort of duty). In testing maxims of the former sort, no particular possible human purposes are considered (though the purposiveness of human acts is presupposed) while in the latter case certain possible purposes—though never those purposes which are simply the desires of agents—are considered.

Another suggestion for deriving a contradiction from the UTC of maxims which are incompatible with duties of justice is put forward both by Dietrichson and by Kemp.[15] They do not believe that it is necessary, despite the arguments for particular duties of justice which Kant gives as instances of the use of Formula I, to invoke the purposiveness of natural laws (let alone their systematic purposiveness) to show how contradictions are derivable from maxims contrary to duties of justice. They both hope to show that one of Kant's examples, that of promising falsely, cannot be conceived as a universal law without contradiction. The argument is put like this by Dietrichson:

. . . . a universal law of nature modeled on the principle of the maxim [of promising falsely to get oneself out of financial difficulties] would be a *self-contradictory law*. Because the very principle of the law would contradict itself, the law in question would be no law at all. —If the world were to be such that everybody who makes promises to get out of a difficult situation would, according to a *natural law* of voluntary action, be absolutely incapable of keeping those promises, no one would take their so-called promises seriously. Such "promises" would be known to be worthless and would therefore not be regarded as *promises*. A universal law of nature modeled on the principle in question would be a law according to which everybody in a certain type of situation would have to *do the impossible*; make promises which he intends to be deceptive, even though he cannot *intend* them to be deceptive, namely because he *knows* that his so-called promises are incapable of deceiving anybody.[16]

[15] P. Dietrichson, "When is a Maxim fully Universalizable?," *Kant-Studien,* Vol. 55, 1964, and J. Kemp, "Kant's Examples of the Categorical Imperative," *Philosophical Quarterly,* Vol. 8, 1958.
[16] P. Dietrichson, pp. 157–58.

Kemp writes more briefly:

> If, *per impossibile,* there were a universal law to this effect [viz. false promising] then there would not be and never would have been any promises . . . but the statement that there is such a law of nature also entails that there are promises. Hence it has contradictory implications . . . [continuing in a footnote] . . . people might have used the expression 'I promise,' but they could not (logically) have used it for the purpose of making a promise; for you cannot (again logically) make a promise if nobody will believe you. Although you could say 'I promise to repay the money' it would be only a statement of intention, not a promise, which requires the existence of a promisee as well as a promiser.[17]

Neither of these passages in fact shows that the UTC of a maxim of false promising is a self-contradictory law of nature. Both derivations of the contradiction require (besides definitions, such as that promises require promisees) the additional premise that it is generally known that everyone is promising falsely. As long as each person imagines that he alone is promising falsely and erroneously accepts others' promises at face value, it will be possible for the law of nature "Everyone will promise falsely" to hold. True, it is implausible that men should not learn from disappointment; but it is an empirical matter if they do so. The hypothetical law of nature under consideration is not *self*-contradictory, but merely incompatible with the fact that men learn from experience. If they did not, false promises might consistently and universally (though pointlessly) be given and accepted.

The Dietrichson/Kemp line of argument is so close to showing that the UTC of the maxim of false promising is self-contradictory that it seems well worth trying to revise it. Is it necessary for the UTC of a maxim incompatible with duty to be shown self-contradictory? Is there a sufficient reason why one should not use true, empirical premises in the derivation of contradictions in such cases?

There are several reasons why such refurbishing may seem impossible. In the first place it has insufficient textual support. While it is true that Kant's example of applications of Formula I appeal frequently to empirical matters,

---

[17] J. Kemp, p. 67. Kemp and Dietrichson both see a contradiction arising from the same conjunction of circumstances: the attempt to make a promise when promises cannot be made since they will not be accepted. They differ in that Dietrichson holds that this shows that the agent's intentions are self contradictory, while Kemp thinks his intentions are adequate and only his performance is a failure. In this Dietrichson is much closer to the interpretation suggested in this section.

his description of the test refers to an *inner* impossibility [18] in nonuniversal-izable maxims. And an inner impossibility is presumably not an incompati-bility between a UTC and some true, but quite extraneous, empirical pre-mise. Further, if we allow that a maxim has been shown contrary to duty whenever we can derive a contradiction from the conjunction of its UTC and true empirical premises, then it will be easy to show some maxims which are *prima facie* maxims of duty are contrary to duty. For example, the maxim "To pay my debts" has the UTC "Everyone will pay his debts." If it is a fact about a given society that not all debtors have the wherewithal to repay what they owe, then they cannot do so, and so a contradiction can be derived from this UTC and one true empirical premise. But perhaps ways can be found to discriminate the sort of empirical fact that is admissible in seeing whether there is any contradiction.

Yet those who advocate this interpretation of the contradiction in concep-tion test concentrate on the example of false promising and fail to discuss what sorts of empirical facts can *generally* be adduced in trying to derive con-tradictions. It does not seem likely that they could provide equally convinc-ing derivations of contradictions from the UTC's of the contraries of other maxims of justice. That they do not consider Kant's other example of an application of this test is not in itself a matter for concern, for that example is intended to show that suicide is contrary to duty. Kant later came to think of suicide as a violation not of a duty of justice but of a duty of virtue, albeit one which requires of us a specific omission. In the *Metaphysik der Sitten* refraining from suicide is an ethical duty of omission. So we would expect not the contradiction in conception test but the contradiction in the will test to show it wrong. Even so there are many duties of justice, other than that of keeping our promises, for which the contradiction in conception test should be a criterion. Kant himself is no help here. In the *Grundlegung* he gives only the example of false promising and the (spurious) example of suicide; in the *Rechtslehre* he is preoccupied with deriving duties of justice, not directly from Formula Ia, but from a very abstract concept of property that he has derived from the Formula of Universal Law via the Universal Principle of Justice. But the contradiction in conception test is also not widely applied by those of Kant's commentators who claim to have found an effective interpretation of the test.

There is good reason for this reticence. When the test is more widely

[18] *G.*, p. 424.

applied, one cannot avoid showing that all sorts of *prima facie* trivial maxims are maxims of duty. Take the maxim "I will receive presents, but not give them." Since gifts must have recipients the UTC of this maxim, "Everyone will receive presents, but nobody will give them," is clearly self-contradictory. We need assume no empirical premises to derive this contradiction and to show this maxim contrary to duty. At least we might be prepared to accept that it is really a maxim of duty not to receive presents unless one gives them. But the same argument can show the maxim "I will give presents but not receive them" self-contradictory, and so contrary to duty. We might perhaps accept that it is a duty to allow others opportunity to be generous and so to accept their gifts—but it hardly seems appropriate that this should be a duty of justice. But the real difficulty is revealed when we consider maxims such as "I will give others cigarettes, but not accept them" or "I will sell others lettuce but not buy it." For these, too, turn out to be contrary to duty. And so do their opposite numbers "I will accept cigarettes from others but not give them" and "I will buy lettuce from others and not sell it." So it would seem that duty requires that all "reciprocal" acts be reciprocated in the most trivial details, if those details are intentional. The Dietrichson/Kemp interpretation of the contradiction in conception test apparently cannot identify all maxims which we (and Kant) would think maxims of justice; but it does select some false positives as maxims of duty.

The problem faced in trying to devise an acceptable interpretation of the contradiction in conception test is then that of finding a test that selects (at least roughly) those maxims which Kant, and we, would probably think maxims of justice; which does not select (many) false positives, and which in some sense shows that there is an *inner* impossibility in the UTC's of maxims contrary to duties of justice. Clearly the derivation of a contradiction from the UTC's of maxims that are contrary to duties of justice is not often possible unless additional empirical premises are used. But which other empirical premises is it legitimate to assume?

Consider the wording of Formulas I and Ia of the Categorical Imperative once again. As first stated, they run, respectively,

I. Act only on that maxim through which you can at the same time will that it should become a universal law.

Ia. Act as if the maxim of your action were to become through your will a universal law of nature.

Two elements in the first of these formulations should be noted. Maxims which are not contrary to duty must be conceivable as a universal law *through* the maxim and *at the same time as* the maxim is held.[19] Both applications of the Formula of Universal Law are tests which an agent applies to his own intentions as expressed in his maxim; even the contradiction in conception test is a test of a consistent will or set of intentions.

In making the contradiction in conception test, two elements are under consideration: a maxim of action and its UTC. We must see, not whether the UTC alone or in conjunction with arbitrarily selected true empirical premises entails a contradiction, but whether the agent can consistently *simultaneously* hold his maxim and will its UTC. But what is meant by willing a hypothetical law of nature? Clearly it is not a matter of whether the agent wants or wishes that the UTC were an actual law of nature. If the contradiction in conception test made such an appeal to inclinations it could not, according to Kant's views, be a test of the rightness, or more generally of the moral acceptability, of maxims. But though an agent does not have to want that the UTC of his maxim become an actual law of nature, he must be able to *intend* that it do so. Since he is not able to legislate or enforce universal laws (whether practical laws or laws of nature) such an intention cannot be realized by an individual agent. Hence the criteria for ascribing such intentions to agents must be rather unusual.

An attribution of the intention that the UTC of a given maxim be universal law is justified if the agent would have that intention if his will were "a will which by all its maxims enacts universal law." [20] This fictitious assumption of a capacity to legislate universally is also indicated in the opening words of Formula Ia, "Act *as if* . . . ." By assuming the fiction that his will is universally legislating, an agent is able to stage a direct confrontation between two intentions: the intention embodied in his maxim and that

[19] Cf. also the renderings of these formulae at *G.*, pp. 434 and 436–37 (twice), *K.P.V.*, p. 30 and *M.S.*, p. 224. In all these the qualification "at the same time" appears, and in some the qualification that the universal law must be willable "through" the agent's maxim.

[20] *G.*, p. 432 ff. This indicates how close to the Formula of Universal Law the Formula of the Kingdom of Ends is, despite its superficial differences. That formula requires us to act so "that the will can regard itself as at the same time making universal law by means of its maxims," *G.*, p. 434. It is no part of this chapter to vindicate Kant's claim that all formulations of the Categorical Imperative are equivalent. But that claim receives some corroboration from the interpretation here given to the Formula of Universal Law.

expressed in its UTC which, *qua* universal legislator, he also intends. If these two intentions are not compatible his maxim is not permissible.

The Formula of Universal Law states in the first place a criterion for coherent intentions, and only via this a test for maxims of duty. This explains why Kant includes the qualification "simultaneously" or "at the same time as" in the formula. Intentions are datable. Unless two intentions are held at the same time, there is no possibility of their being inconsistent. If the presence or absence of a contradiction between intentions is to discriminate maxims of duty from other maxims, then one must assume that the intentions can be ascribed to the same agent at the same time.

One might, however, wonder whether there can ever by any contradiction between intending to do some act and the intention that everyone similarly situated do the same act. If we consider the two intentions schematically it would seem impossible. For they would be, respectively:

(3′) I will – – – – if · · · ·

(6) Everyone will – – – – if · · · ·

Rather it seems that (3′) is an instantiation of (6), and that no contradiction would ever be possible. But to draw this conclusion is to take too limited a view of what it is to have an intention. If I intend to, say, rob a bank, I intend also some sufficient set of conditions to realize my ends and the normal, predictable results of the success of my intended action.[21] For instance, I intend the continued existence of the bank I plan to rob, that I be neither discovered nor interrupted during the theft, and that I shall use or enjoy the fruits of the theft. These are not separate intentions which a person who intends to rob a bank may or may not have; they are part and parcel of normal intentions to rob banks. Similarly if I intend *qua* universal legislator that everyone should rob some bank, then I must also intend some conditions sufficient for them to do so and the normal and predictable results of their suc-

---

[21] Though it is hard to find any objection to either of these amplifications of what is involved in intending to do some act, it is also hard to produce a convincing justification for either. Kant held that the requirement that one intend some sufficient means to an act intended was, at least in a loose sense, analytic of the notion of rationality. Cf. *G.*, p. 417 " 'If I fully will the effect, I also will the action required for it' is analytic," and also L. W. Beck *A Commentary on Kant's Critique of Practical Reason*, pp. 84–88. We can call this the Principle of Hypothetical Imperatives. The requirement that one intend the normal and predictable results of one's acts might equally loosely, but convincingly, be defended as analytic of the notion of rationality.

ceeding in doing so. But I cannot intend that everybody be not interrupted or discovered in their theft from a bank and be able to use or enjoy the fruits of their theft. I must intend the normal and predictable results of the success of any course of action which I intend, and the normal result of everyone's stealing from banks is that banks will take ever greater precautions to impede and discover thieves and to prevent them using or enjoying their loot. Failing successful prevention, banks, as we know them, would close down.

I cannot intend a system of nature in which everybody does what I do. So if my maxim is to rob a bank I cannot universalize it. In my capacity as universal legislator, I would intend that all theft from banks and, hence, my theft from a bank and the use and enjoyment of its results become increasingly difficult and eventually impossible; yet in my private capacity I intend that my theft from a bank be feasible and successful. If an agent does act on the maxim of robbing a bank, or on any other maxim whose universalization would require him to have self-contradictory intentions, then the outcome will be ". . . no contradiction, but rather an opposition to the precept of reason (antagonismus), whereby the universality of the principle (universalitas) is turned to mere generality (generalitas)." [22]

In such cases we intend that we should be an exception to the universal law, and that the law be not really universal. In the example given, we intend both that banks continue to exist in their present form, as part of the necessary conditions for the robberies we intend, and that banks do not continue to exist in their present form, as part of the normal and predictable results of the robberies we intend. Rational beings cannot intend a society of bank robbers.

The derivation of a contradiction from the intentions of an agent trying to universalize his maxim of bank robbing depends upon the generality of that maxim. But each bank robbery can be described and may be intended much more specifically. Suppose a person with red hair named Ignatz MacGillycuddy (in honor of Singer) intends to rob a bank exactly northeast of his house at 5 P.M. on a Thursday. He discovers that he can without contradiction intend a system of nature in which any red-headed person named Ignatz MacGillycuddy who has a bank exactly northeast of his house robs that bank at 5 P.M. on a Thursday, and that his own robbery take place in such a system of nature. Is this robbery then not forbidden? Does Kant face an analogue of Singer's problem of invertible principles?

Kant's problem is quite different from Singer's. A person cannot simply

[22] *G.*, p. 424.

claim a highly specific maxim, as in the Ignatz MacGillycuddy example. He must, in fact, intend his act to be contingent on those restrictions and not merely pursued by these means if he is to hold his maxim is specific and so universalizable. He must demonstrate (perhaps only to his own satisfaction) that he would drop his project of bank robbing if his hair turned gray or 5 P.M. passed or the bank turned out to be north-northeast of his house and so on. On the whole, I believe, agents who are honest will not claim to have highly specific maxims. They know that when they claim that they will rob a bank of a specified sort in a specified way, etc., their project is not really contingent upon these specifications. As always, Kant places great reliance on agents being honest and careful in stating what it is that they intend to do. In general, the contradiction in conception test is extremely sensitive to the details of agents' maxims. Some of the consequences of this sensitivity will be discussed in chapters 6 and 7.

Confirmation for this interpretation of the contradiction in conception test can be found in the restricted version of the Categorical Imperative which Kant calls the Universal Principle of Justice. The clearer version of this principle runs: "Act externally in such a way that the free use of your will is compatible with the freedom of everybody according to universal law." [23] This formula seems to introduce a novel element in its explicit restriction to external acts. But this is not, in fact, an added restriction. The test for contradictions in conception as here interpreted could not show any act but an external one forbidden. Internal acts are by definition ones which do not affect others directly (they may presumably affect others indirectly by changing the agent's character). So if I can intend to do an internal act myself, I can also intend all others to do so.

So the Universal Principle of Justice can be reduced without distortion to "act so that the free use of your will is compatible with the freedom of everyone according to universal law." The universal law here envisaged is presumably a law of freedom, not of nature. But the results of this test are, nevertheless, the same as those of the contradiction in conception test as interpreted here. If I assume that everybody exercises his freedom by adopting the maxim I have adopted, then I must assume that the natural law expressed in the UTC of my maxim is true. But if I believe that a natural law holds, I must also believe that some conditions sufficient for its holding obtain and that the normal and predictable consequences of its holding are

[23] *M.S.,* p. 231.

realized. Only if my own maxim is compatible with these beliefs would it be compatible with intending the UTC of my maxim *qua* universal legislator; so the two tests are equivalent.

This interpretation of the contradiction in conception test proposes a far from mechanical method for determining whether acting on a maxim is compatible with duty. But the method is still relatively clear and definite. It asks whether we can simultaneously intend to do *x* (assuming that we must intend some set of conditions sufficient for the successful carrying out of our intentions and the normal and predictable results of successful execution) and intend everyone else to do *x* (assuming again that we must intend some conditions sufficient for the successful execution of their intentions and the normal and predictable results of such execution). No appeal is made in this interpretation of the test to particular desires or inclinations or to particular empirical situations. Naturally an agent who is working out what his intentions commit him to must take certain empirical facts into account. But a limit is placed on the sort of empirical material which may be adduced in testing a maxim by the relevance of the empirical material to the coherence of the agent's intentions. There are still good reasons for calling the contradictions which may be derived from applications of this test "inner impossibilities." They mark an incoherence *within* the intentions of a particular agent.

Only given a certain background of empirical facts can an agent's intention to do an act be determinate. For only given these can he work out whether there is some feasible means for executing his intention and what the normal and predictable results of successful execution of the intention would be. But just which sorts of facts may or must an agent assume to see what exactly his intentions commit him to?

If this cannot be stated carefully we shall be back with a problem like that of providing a relevant description of an act. Is it, for instance, permissible for an agent testing the maxim of embezzlement to assume as an empirical fact that he will not be apprehended? Or is this not part of the normal and predictable results of successful embezzling? The answer in such cases is that he may do so only if he assumes also that, if everyone else embezzles, they will not be apprehended. The only sense in which Kant does rely upon the notion of a system of nature in the statement of the contradiction in conception test is that he requires that we ask "Whether if the action you propose should take place by a law of nature of which you yourself were a part you could regard it as possible through your will." [24] Appeal cannot be made to empirical facts such as that not everyone will do likewise or that this act will (or will not) serve as a bad example. For the hypothesis against which a maxim is tested is precisely that others do the same, whether or not because of the example given.

But this is not a sufficient restriction on the sorts of empirical circumstance which a man may assume in determining what his intentions commit him to. He must assume, not only that he belongs to the same system of nature as others, but, if he is seeing whether his maxim is a maxim of human duty, he must assume that he belongs to that system of nature to which men belong. He cannot, for instance, assume that a duplicate of stolen property is somehow miraculously presented to the owner, who is therefore not deprived while the thief enjoys the original. If we did live in such a system of nature, precautions against theft would presumably never be taken and the maxim of thieving could consistently be universalized. But this is no reason for rejecting the interpretation of the test. One would not expect the moral status of theft to be the same in such a system of nature as it is in our own.

Tests of the capacity of maxims to guide any human moral choices must assume those natural laws in whose context all human society operates—that men are mortal and learn from experience; that material goods are not infinitely abundant and are desired, and additional specific laws of this sort. No doubt it is not entirely clear which generalizations about the human condition are laws of nature, but this is a question which judgment is not powerless to solve. The fact that agents testing the rightness and moral worth of acts done or proposed have to make judgments of this sort does, however, show once again how far from mechanical this test is. To apply it fairly, agents must assess their intentions and the probable results of their success with complete honesty. This fact may account for the enormous stress which Kant places on duties such as integrity and conscientiousness.

Though I have now given one account of an application of the test for duties of justice, I have not yet described a general method for determining the legal status of an act. In the example considered, the agent could not consistently universalize his intentions, and so his maxim (of robbing a bank) was contrary to duty and acts conforming to it forbidden. But what is the legal status of an act whose maxim can be consistently universalized? How do we tell whether it is obligatory or merely permissible?

[24] *K.P.V.*, p. 69.

Kant does not spell out procedures for determining the legal status of acts at any point. But such procedures are implicit in what he writes, and are guaranteed by their foundation in deontic logic. In the case of a maxim that can be consistently universalized, a second application of the contradiction in conception test to the maxim's contrary [25] is needed to determine the deontic status of acts conforming to the maxim. If an agent's maxim is a specification of (3), of form

C. To do A if B,

and no contradiction emerges when C is universalized, then the same test must be applied to

D. To omit A if B.

If the test now yields a contradiction, then it is forbidden to omit A if B and consequently obligatory to do A if B. If no contradiction emerges from either the test of C or the test of D then it is merely permissible to do A if B.

I have so far considered contradictions derivable when an agent universalizes his maxim, those derivable when he universalizes its contrary, and the case when none is derivable from either procedure. Since there are precisely three distinct legal statuses which an act can have, it would be convenient if there were also precisely three outcomes from applying the contradiction in conception test to any maxim and its contrary. Unfortunately, there would seem to be a fourth possibility: the case where a contradiction is derivable both from a universalized maxim and from its universalized contrary. One might be inclined to dismiss this as a case which would never arise. If maxims had all to be syntactically simple it would not arise. But there is no

---

[25] Speaking strictly, it is not the maxim's contrary which we test in those (typical) cases where the agent's maxim is of form (2′), (3) or (3′). No distinction can be made between the contrary and the contradictory of unquantified, nonmodal formulas of this sort. But I shall call the pair of maxims which must be tested in any complete application of the contradiction in conception test *contraries,* because their UTC's are contraries, and not contradictories. Given two maxims and their UTC's, such as:

    E. I will do A if B   F. I will omit A if B
    G. Everyone will do A if B   H. Everyone will omit A if B

where G and H are contraries and are, respectively, the UTC's of E and F. I shall speak of E and F also as contraries.

such requirement. And so one of the classes of maxims which gave trouble to the Kemp/Dietrichson interpretation of Kantian universality raises just this problem for this interpretation of the contradiction in conception test. There are maxims which cannot be consistently universalized and whose contraries also cannot be consistently universalized. Such are maxims of nonreciprocal action. Consider the example.

1. I will buy clockwork trains but not sell them.

In testing this maxim an agent must see whether *qua* universal legislator he could intend

2. Everyone will buy clockwork trains but not sell them.

Clearly he cannot intend 2, since all purchases require simultaneous sales. But a similar conclusion follows from attempting to universalize the contrary of 1, which is

3. I will omit to buy clockwork trains, but I will not omit to sell them.

This has the UTC

4. Nobody will buy clockwork trains but everyone will sell them.

Like 2, 4 cannot consistently be intended by an agent. Similar arguments can be applied to other maxims of nonreciprocal action.

What ethical sense can be made of this situation? It seems as though the contradiction in conception test has succeeded in showing acts conforming to maxims such as 1 both obligatory and forbidden, while such acts seem for other reasons to be merely permissible. No help is to be had from Kant on this point. He seems not to have considered such maxims. But, without a solution to the case where an agent can universalize neither his maxim nor its contrary, Kant's test procedure for duties of justice fails to determine the deontic status of all acts.

Fortunately, a fairly plausible solution to the antinomy of acts can be shown to be both forbidden and obligatory. This solution is suggested by Singer's discussion of invertible applications of the generalization argument.[26] Such applications, it will be remembered, are ones which show both

[26] M. Singer, pp. 71–80.

an act and its omission wrong. Singer holds that these applications do not lead to "morally determinate" results. To know the status of a particular act falling under a principle which does not lead to morally determinate results, one must assess the act under a different description.

Kant's ethical theory cannot take Singer's way out. Kant assumes that the composite act description of the agent's maxim is in all cases the act description under which moral assessment is to be made. So a rather different convention must be adopted to complete this interpretation of the contradiction in conception test. In those cases where neither a maxim nor its contrary can be consistently universalized, acts according with the maxim, or with its contrary, will be classified as merely permissible. The justification for this convention is simply that it fits in coherently with the rest of the interpretation given to the contradiction in conception test, and that the resulting classification of maxims and acts is intuitively acceptable. To classify acts conforming to maxims of nonreciprocal action as "both forbidden and obligatory" would not have been coherent; to classify them either as obligatory or as forbidden would not have been intuitively acceptable. This move is, of course, a shift from exegesis to reconstruction.

We are now in a position to describe a complete method for testing a maxim by the contradiction in conception test. In any such test an agent must check first whether he can without contradiction intend to act on the maxim and intend its UTC to hold as a natural law, and second, whether he can without contradiction intend to act on the contrary of the maxim and intend its UTC to hold as a natural law. In each case, intending a maxim or intending a natural law is incomplete if the agent does not intend some means sufficient for his intention being realized and the normal and predictable consequences of its realization. To go through this procedure is to check whether a maxim and its contrary can be universalized without contradiction. If the procedure shows that both can be universalized or that neither can be, acts conforming either to the maxim or to its contrary are merely permissible. If only the maxim cannot be universalized, acts conforming to it are forbidden; if only the contrary cannot be universalized, acts conforming to the maxim are obligatory.

Although this test has been described as one carried out by an agent assessing the deontic status of his own acts (performed or proposed), it is open to others to apply the same procedure.[27] They need only discover the agent's maxim—whether by questioning, by observation, or by some combination of

[27] But see chapter 7, section I, for more on this.

these—to be able to go through the same procedure. Given a maxim it is a mechanical matter to formulate its UTC, its contrary, and the contrary's UTC, and a matter for skill and judgment of which the agent has no monopoly to check whether either the maxim or its contrary can be consistently universalized.

The plausibility of this interpretation of the contradiction in conception test has so far only been indicated by showing that it rules that bank robbing is forbidden, and that it does not (if we add one plausible convention to the test) show that all reciprocal acts must be reciprocated in the most trivial details. Some further examples can show its discriminating powers.

Consider the maxim of false promising, with UTC "Everyone will promise falsely." No agent can consistently intend the latter to hold as a law of nature of a system of nature of which he is a part and in which he intends to promise falsely. In promising falsely he intends the normal, predictable result of successfully doing the act—successful deception. He intends that there be a level of general confidence which will lead to his promise being believed. But if the UTC were a law of nature, then, for the reasons Kemp and Dietrichson indicate, successful deception would be an increasingly unlikely result of false promising, since public confidence would diminish and eventually vanish. The predictable result of the UTC of this maxim being a law of nature in the system of nature to which men belong would be that there would be no means by which the agent could succeed in acting on his maxim. Only if the agent were to postulate a system of nature in which men do not learn from experience could he consistently intend the maxim and its UTC. On the other hand, he can consistently universalize the maxim of keeping his promises. Thus, false promising is forbidden. With slight changes this argument can show why specific sorts of promise breaking and deception are forbidden.

Or take the maxim of growing food, with UTC "Everyone will grow food." This principle gave Singer some difficulty, since his test of the deontic status of acts makes it depend on the desirability of the consequences of universal principles, and it is clearly neither desirable that everyone grow food nor desirable that nobody do so. It is from this example that he develops the notion of an invertible application of the generalization argument and of morally indeterminate acts. No such difficulties arise with the Kantian test. I can consistently intend that I and everybody grow food (once most of the world was like that). And I can consistently intend that I and all others omit to grow food. It is true that the absence of food would lead to our starvation, but starving people can omit acts as well as the best fed. So I can consistently intend some means to and the predictable results of myself and all others not growing food. Growing food as such is, therefore, merely permissible, though there may be particular circumstances under which growing food is either forbidden or obligatory.

Some problems might be raised about the discriminating power of the contradiction in conception test as applied to maxims of nonreciprocal action. While the convention adopted—that acts whose maxims and contrary maxims can neither of them be consistently universalized are merely permissible—seems to yield intuitively acceptable results for the cases like buying but not selling clockwork trains, one might feel that at a more general level reciprocity is a duty. Though we do not feel that it is a duty to give the same items or sorts of items as we receive, to produce just what we consume, or to buy just what we sell, we do feel, in general terms, that exchanges ought to be fair. Yet the convention suggested will not show even very general maxims of reciprocal action such as "To repay favors received" or "Not to consume unless I produce" maxims of justice. But duties of justice are not all the duties there are. Kant classifies gratitude as a duty of virtue; he does not discuss reciprocity on commercial transactions because, as a liberal, he thinks that due observation of promises and contracts is a sufficient guarantee of justice in that sphere. But it is possible that the contradiction in conception test applied with an eye to certain laws of nature that Kant, with his radical view of human freedom, rather neglected (such as that men's tastes and preferences are formed by their education and class) would justify some rather more "Aristotelian" duties of justice—a duty to charge fair prices, to give appropriate amounts in relation to one's income, and so on.

We can also now see in detail why refraining from suicide is not a duty of justice. The maxim "I will end my life when I want to" and its UTC "Everyone will end his life when he wants to" can simultaneously be intended. I can without self-contradiction, intend everyone to have the means to suicide and the consequent extinction of the human species. There is no inner impossibility in intending a system in which we act like lemmings.

On the other hand, a maxim of unrestricted killing is shown self-contradictory. It might be "I shall kill others without reason" with UTC "Everybody will kill others without reason." If I intend to kill others without reason, then I intend to survive myself to do so; but if I intend everybody to

be engaged in random killing then I, too, am at risk. The normal and predictable results of generalized killing is not a means a rational agent could
choose in order to act on the maxim of killing others.

An application of the contradiction in conception test can also be used to
show that it is a duty of justice to obey the civil authorities. The result is a
version of a "state of nature" argument, but one which refers simply to the
fact that men have ends, not to specific human desires. If an agent's maxim
is "I will not obey the civil authorities," and its UTC "Everyone will omit to
obey the civil authorities," then he must intend both of these. But this he
cannot do. If he were a part of a system of nature in which the UTC held as a
law of nature, there would, for Hobbesian reasons, be no possibility of pursuing any end with a reasonable prospect of security and success. No agent
can consistently intend himself and others to pursue a line of action in a system of nature which tends to disrupt all planed and systematic action. So I
could not consistently intend my own maxim of disobedience and its UTC.
On the other hand, the maxim of obeying the civil authorities can be consistently universalized. It should be noted that this argument shows only that
it is forbidden to disobey the civil authorities in general; whether there is or
is not a right of revolution or of civil disobedience in various specific circumstances would require further tests of more specific maxims.[28]

In these examples some of the power of this interpretation of the contradiction in conception test can be seen. But the examples given do not have
individual textual corroboration. Nor have I considered all the examples
Kant does give. Some of the reasons for this have already been mentioned.
Suicide is not, in fact, an example of a duty of justice; the arrangement of
the *Rechtslehre* means that Kant is never there engaged in deriving individual
duties of justice from the Categorical Imperative or directly from the Universal Principle of Justice. But it seems that I have also dealt very cavalierly
with the one undoubted example of the justification of a duty of justice
which Kant does give—the argument that false promising is forbidden.[29]
But another look at that argument shows that it is not so far removed from
the pattern of argument here proposed as attempts to assimilate it to other
interpretations might suggest.

[28] For a discussion of Kant's mixed views on the French Revolution cf. L. W.
Beck, "Kant and the Right of Revolution," and S. Axinn, "Kant, Authority and the
French Revolution," both in *Journal of the History of Ideas,* Vol. 32, 1971.
[29] *G.,* p. 422.

Apart from one reference to "the purpose of promising," on which the Paton/Beck interpretation hinges, Kant's argument is close both to Kemp/Dietrichson and to the present approach. He writes:

I then see straight away that this maxim {that of false promising} can never rank as a universal law and be self-consistent, but must necessarily contradict itself. For the universality of a law that everyone believing himself to be in need may make any promise he pleases with the intention not to keep it would make promising, and the very purpose of promising, itself impossible, since no one would believe he was being promised anything, but would laugh at promises of this kind as empty shams.[30]

Kemp and Dietrichson think that a contradiction is to be got from the UTC of a maxim of false promising. Kant, in fact, makes it clear that it is the conjunction of the maxim and its UTC which is inconsistent. Universal law must be willed *through* the maxim. "The universality of a law that everyone believing himself in need may make any promise he pleases with the intention not to keep it would make promising itself impossible." This would not be contradictory were there no promises actual or proposed. But of course we know that there is at least one promise proposed from the agent's maxim. That maxim is, therefore, an essential element in the derivation of a contradiction.

The element that must be added to Kant's argument is that both the formulas, the maxim, and its UTC, must be intended by the agent simultaneously. It is the fact that they are intentions that makes it possible to determine which empirical considerations may be adduced in deriving a contradiction and which may not be. The consideration which Kant adduces—the collapse of trust if the UTC became law—is one which any agent intending the UTC must also intend. It is the normal and predictable result of such a law characterizing a system of nature such as the one in which men live. So the *Grundlegung* application of the contradiction in conception test to show false promising contrary to duty is an incomplete application of the test with a few redundant elements; but it is not a different pattern of argument.

The contradiction in conception test, which Kant's commentators have often thought clear but fruitless, is quite fruitful. Whether this interpretation is clear or not is largely a matter of semantics. It is not simple; it is definite. My aim is now to provide an interpretation of the contradiction in the will test which also builds on the Kantian text, is also fruitful, and also definite.

[30] *Ibid.*

II *Contradiction in the Will*

Kant's test for the maxims of duties of wide obligation is in a way misleadingly named. The contradiction in conception test is itself a test of coherent intentions, of coherent willing. But it is not a test which relies on any assumptions about the *objects* of agents' wills, about their ends or purposes. It does assume that agents have ends and that they intend the normal and predictable results of acts they intend. And these results will be at least part of their purpose, unless their purpose is just to do the act; i.e., unless their complete maxim of ends is of form (4'). But purposes as such are not involved in the contradiction in conception test, while they are essential in the contradiction in the will test for duties of virtue.

The contradiction in the will test depends on showing that there are certain ends which it is a duty for men to have. But the very notion of an obligatory end has seemed to many incompatible with central parts of Kant's ethical theory. Does not Kant say that ethics must not depend on any human desires? So, before one can turn to any of Kant's arguments that there must be obligatory ends, or to his arguments identifying specific obligatory ends, it is essential to show that the notion of an obligatory end is consistent with the rest of his ethical theory.

Kant defines an end as "an object of the power of choice (of a rational being) through the thought of which choice is determined to an action to produce this object." [31] The evidence that a given state of affairs, *s,* is an end for an agent is that the agent does something or other to achieve *s* (unless no course of action is available to him, and known by him to be available). The act he does can be explained (in part) by showing that *s* is an end for him. The most obvious sort of end is an end which is wanted or desired. The evidence that an agent wants *s* is that he does something to achieve *s* (if this is open to him), and his act can be explained (in part) by pointing out that he wants *s*. But throughout his writings on ethics Kant maintains that the wants and desires of particular agents have no bearing on the moral acceptability of their acts. "All practical principles which presuppose an *object* [material] of the faculty of desire as the determining ground of the will are without exception empirical and can furnish no practical laws." [32] Hence his claim that there can be ends that are obligatory, which

[31] *M.S.,* p. 380; cf. *ibid.,* p. 383.   [32] *K.P.V.,* p. 21; cf. *G.,* p. 400.

agents ought to adopt in their "maxims of ends," depends on there being ends that are not the wants and desires of particular agents. There must be at least some "objects of the power of rational choice" which are not also "objects of the faculty of desire" if Kant's doctrine of obligatory ends is to be consistent with the rest of his ethical theory.

A satisfactory interpretation of Kant's ethical theory, and in particular of his *Metaphysik der Sitten,* requires that there be ends other than those desired. Kant assumes that there are, as is shown by the frequency with which he speaks of "adopting ends" or "choosing ends" and of "ends which we ought to have." We do not adopt or choose desires, we have them. And if there are any desires which we ought to have, then we cannot acquire them by any direct process of choice, but only by some sort of education or cultivation of ourselves. Our duties to adopt ends are not duties to have certain desires. A duty of love, for example does not require that we want to treat others in a certain way. Feelings are irrelevant to duty. A duty of love "must rather be taken as a maxim of benevolence (practical love) which has beneficence as its consequence." [33] Similarly the most general duties of virtue cannot be duties to want our own perfection and others' happiness.

The only passage I know which might be taken as meaning that Kant thinks that no ends can be obligatory is in the *Grundlegung,* where he writes: "Moral worth can be found nowhere but *in the principle of the will* irrespective of the ends that can be brought about by such an action." [34] But this passage in fact say no more than that *if* an end has any bearing on the moral worth of an act, then this end must be one mentioned in the agents' principle of the will—i.e., in his maxim of ends. It is only ends intended, and not the incidental results of action, that can have any bearing on the moral worth of acts. This passage is quite consistent with there being obligatory ends; only these ends must be neither ends which are merely desired nor unintended results of action.

Another version of the same alleged inconsistency is sometimes seen in what Kant says about formal and material requirements on moral principles. If morality requires that the will "be determined by the formal principle of volition when an act is done from duty, where . . . every material principle is taken away from it," [35] then how can there be obligatory ends? For are not ends the matter of the will and principles involving ends (i.e., maxims of ends) material principles? But this difficulty too vanishes when one pays at-

[33] *M.S.,* p. 448.   [34] *G.,* p. 400.   [35] *Ibid.*

tention to the distinction between the objects of the faculty of desire or subjective ends, and the objects of the faculty of choice or ends in general. Only
the former are excluded from maxims of duty; provided they are excluded,
the maxim meets Kant's condition for being formal: "Practical principles are
formal if they abstract from all subjective ends; they are *material,* on the other
hand, if they are based on such ends and consequently on certain compul-
sions." [36]

Kant does not always make it entirely explicit whether he is talking of
ends in general or of ends desired,[37] but the context usually makes it sufficiently clear. There is no conflict between the exclusion of material ends
from moral maxims and the mention of ends in these maxims.

These considerations show only that Kant may consistently claim that there
are ends other than the ends desired which may be relevant to the moral assessment of acts. They do not show that there must be obligatory ends, nor
that our own perfection and others' happiness are such ends, but only that
there is no *prima facie* reason for thinking that the first principle of the doctrine of virtue is an inadmissible specification of the Categorical Imperative.
In the next chapter I hope to link the doctrine of obligatory ends with the
theory that moral worth depends on the motive with which an act is done.
In this chapter my aim is more modest. I shall try to give an interpretation
of the contradiction in the will test, in the light of the first principle of ethics, which has textual support as well as practical implications.

In structure, the test for maxims of virtue is the same as that for maxims
of justice. This is not surprising since both tests are applications of the
Formula of Universal Law. But the point of application of the two tests is
different. Acts violate duties of virtue if their maxim of ends, not their
maxim of action, cannot be consistently universalized. So an application of
the test for a maxim of virtue begins by considering the agent's complete
maxim of ends, of form

(4) To − − − − if · · · · in order to ———,

and forming its UTC,

(7) Everyone will − − − − if · · · · in order to ———.

[36] *G.,* p. 426.   [37] Cf. e.g. *M.S.,* p. 375.

Assuming that acts done on such a maxim violate no duty of justice, any contradiction derivable from (4) and (7) must depend on the introduction of the purposive component "in order to ———." There are two ways in which such a component could lead to a contradiction. The first case would be where the act described in the composite act description could not lead to the end mentioned in the purposive component. In this case an act done on the maxim would be irrational and might yet have a permissible or even obligatory end. Though it is essential to consider which maxims of action are compatible with which maxims of ends for a complete statement of the contradiction in the will test, such compatibility in no way guarantees that the end aimed at is permissible, let alone obligatory. In determining which are maxims of virtue it is essential to establish first which ends—if any—are obligatory. So the contradiction in the will test must derive contradictions only from the purposive components of maxims of ends; i.e., only from *incomplete* maxims of ends and not from an incompatibility between act and end. We must begin by considering

(4″) To do/omit what is needed in order to ———,

with UTC of form

(7′) Everyone will do/omit what is needed in order to ———.

As in the case of the contradiction in conception test, it seems at first as though a contradiction could never be derived from a maxim of ends of form (4″) and its UTC of form (7′) unless the specification of the purposive component, "———," were itself incoherent. But in such a case Kant would have held that the agent did not really have any maxim of ends to which the test could be applied. The contradiction in the will test is intended to show certain coherent purposes forbidden, and others either merely permissible or obligatory.

As in the contradiction in conception test, the actual working out of any application of the test depends on the fact that maxims of ends, like maxims of action, stand in definite logical relations with one another.

An agent may have any of four policies with regard to a given end, x. He may intend to do some of what is needed to achieve x, or some of what is needed to prevent x; he may intend to neglect everything which is needed to achieve x, or everything which is needed to prevent x. However no maxim of ends has the form "I will do everything which is needed to achieve (or prevent) x," since we cannot ever do all those acts which would achieve a given end, since doing some sufficient set of acts will always preclude doing other sets of sufficient acts. Nor does any nontrivial maxim of ends have the form "I will neglect some of what is needed to achieve (or prevent) x." For, once again, we *must* neglect at least some of the acts which are needed to achieve or prevent x, since doing some of them always precludes doing others.[38]

The four schematic maxims of ends which are possible and nontrivial may be arranged in a square of opposition.

A. To do some of what is needed to achieve x.

B. To do some of what is needed to prevent x.

C. To neglect everything needed to prevent x.

D. To neglect everything needed to achieve x.

The following logical relations hold between these four policies. Any agent choosing a policy with respect to x must have one, but only one, of each of the pairs of contradictory maxims A and D, B and C, as a maxim of ends. No agent can have both C and D as maxims of ends. An agent may have both A and B as maxims of ends, and if he has any policy must have one of these. An agent who has C as a maxim of ends also intends A; one who has D as a maxim of ends also intends B.

The actual test procedure can now be examined, beginning as in the discussion of the test for duties of justice, with the examples Kant gives in the *Grundlegung*. In his examples of applications of the Formula of Universal Law, Kant discusses the duty to develop one's talents and the duty to help others in need. If these are to be shown obligatory ends, then a contradiction should be derivable from an attempt to will as universal law a maxim of neglecting these ends.

If there is any duty to help others in need, Kant points out, it must be a wide duty. We can quite consistently intend a system of nature in which men do not help one another. It is not contrary to any duty of justice to act on the maxim

[38] Cf. the discussion of possible principles of right, chapter 1, p. 6.

1. To neglect everything needed to help the needy.

We can consistently will 1, and its UTC,

2. Everyone will neglect everything needed to help the needy.

For 2 is a possible law of a nature of which I might will to be a part consistently with all those considerations which may be relevantly adduced in a contradiction in conception test. But certain other considerations are relevant in the contradiction in the will test.

One necessary fact about men is, Kant thinks, here relevant. This is that men have ends. This is not a fact that anybody would be inclined to dispute, though the basis for calling it "necessary" may be unclear.[39] I do not propose to investigate that claim of Kant's. But once this fact is taken as a premise, a contradiction may quite readily be deduced from 1 and 2. If men have ends they must, by the Principle of Hypothetical Imperatives (which Kant thinks is analytic), will some sufficient means to those ends. But if I will whatever means are needed to achieve whatever ends I may have, then I must will that, should I be unable to achieve my ends by my unaided efforts, I should be given assistance. I must will to be helped if in need. But if I will this in my private capacity, I cannot also will 2.

The contradiction in the will is a contradiction between a maxim which any human agent must have to be rational, and the UTC of the proposed maxim of neglecting some things needed to help any other in need. It should be noted that this argument shows only that a maxim of giving *no* help to *any* other in need is contrary to duty. The UTC of an intention to neglect everything needed to help the needy commits an agent to the intention that others neglect some things needed to help him in need. Complete lack of beneficence is contrary to duty, but we do not have a duty to help all who need help. Beneficence may be selective without violation of duty. Nor do

---

[39] The contradiction in conception test, of course, also relies on this premise, but for a very different purpose. There certain laws of nature were assumed in order to determine what various intentions would commit an agent to. Should men come to live in a very different system of nature, these premises could not be assumed. But Kant does not think the premise that men have ends could ever be dropped. Indeed the very use of the premise in a test of the moral status of ends assumes that the agent testing his maxim has at least one end.

we have a duty to give all necessary help to any one of those in need. Beneficence may also be partial without violation of duty. Duty requires only the adoption of the contrary of 1, "I will do some of what is needed to help the needy."

The argument, incidentally, also enables Kant to show reciprocity of help a duty without showing that reciprocal acts ought to be reciprocated in the merest details.

The example of developing our own talents has been left till last because it has one peculiarity. Although the argument establishing that it is an obligatory end can fit the very same pattern as the argument showing that it is an obligatory end to help others in need, it also fits into a simpler pattern. It is not essential to make any reference to the UTC of a maxim of neglecting all one's talents to show that this maxim of ends is contrary to duty. A contradiction can be derived from the conjunction of the agent's maxim of neglect and the fact that men have ends. But this anomaly is, in fact, what we might expect of a duty that can be carried out whether or not there are any other agents. Even in a system of nature of which we were the sole human members we would have opportunity to develop our talents, whereas we would have no opportunity to help others.

The derivation of a contradiction proceeds as follows: given a maxim,

3. I will neglect everything needed in order to develop my talents,

with UTC

4. Everyone will neglect everything needed to develop his talents,

Kant points out that there is no contradiction in the idea of a system of nature in which men entirely neglect their talents. But he claims that there is a contradiction in a rational agent's willing to be part of such a system. Rational beings have ends; they also will some sufficient means to these ends, and the development of some talents is a part of the means to ends of any sort. So rational agents must make it an end to develop at least some of their own talents. If they do not have this end, they cannot claim to have any other end. "For as a rational being he necessarily wills that all his powers should be developed, since they serve him and are given him for all sorts of ends." [40]

[40] G., p. 423.

But the conclusion that all rational agents will to develop some talents con-tradicts both 3 and 4. Hence, neglecting everything needed to develop some talents is impermissible, and so it is obligatory to do what is needed to de-velop some talents. It is optional from the point of view of duty which tal-ents we develop to what extent. But we may not do nothing. What we do must depend on our situation.[41]

So far I have shown that the contradiction in the will test can be used to substantiate Kant's claim that developing some talents and helping some others in need are obligatory ends. But developing some talents is only part of developing one's perfection. Perfection includes moral perfection. And helping those in need is only part of promoting others' happiness. Respect and sympathy as well as beneficence are said to be duties of virtue. Kant does not try in the *Grundlegung* to establish the two most general duties of virtue, i.e., the two obligatory ends of the *Metaphysik der Sitten,* by applying the Formula of Universal Law. When he comes to applying the Formula of the End in Itself, on the other hand, he does argue that we have a duty to promote our own perfection and others' happiness in general. The arguments used in the *Metaphysik der Sitten* to establish these obligatory ends are also not applications of the contradiction in the will test, but the test can be used for this purpose.

To neglect one's own perfection in general is to neglect both one's moral perfection and the development of one's talents. The latter sort of neglect has already been shown contrary to duty. So it remains to consider neglect of cultivation of moral perfection. Kant thinks that there is only one "moral perfection" or "moral talent": a strength of will which an agent manifests in his ability to do his duty without any further incentives, simply because it is his duty.[42] This strength of will is manifested whenever an agent acts on a maxim of virtue, and whenever he acts not merely according to but out of a duty of, justice. It is the constant formal element in all acts done on a maxim of virtue.[43] The maxim to which the contradiction in conception test must be applied is therefore

---

[41] Cf. *M.S.,* p. 391. "Then too, the different situations in which men may find themselves make a man's choice of the sort of occupation for which he should cul-tivate his talents quite arbitrary. With regard to natural perfection, accordingly, reason gives no law for actions but only a law for the maxims of actions, which runs as follows: 'Cultivate your powers of mind and body so that they are fit to realize any end you can come upon,' for it cannot be said which of these could, at some time, become yours."

[42] *M.S.,* pp. 391, 446.   [43] *Ibid.,* p. 404.

5. I will neglect to do everything needed to develop my moral strength of will.

If an agent has this maxim, then, since he must will the means to his ends, he cannot will any end for which developing one's strength of will is an essential means. But developing one's strength of will is a necessary means to one end only: that of acting virtuously or doing one's duty not for any further end but for its own sake, and we know from the previous argument that there is at least one duty of virtue. Acquiring a capacity for any sort of act is always an essential means to doing that act unless the capacity is inborn, which moral strength of will is not.

From the premises that there are some duties of virtue and that agents must will some sufficient means to any ends they desire, the conclusion that developing one's capacity for moral action is required by duty easily follows. Whatever other conditions may be needed for virtuous action, the cultivation of a capacity for such action is clearly a part of any sufficient set of conditions. Moral as well as natural perfection must be cultivated if one is to act dutifully. Perfection of oneself in general is a duty.

The other gap between Kant's examples of applications of the Formula of Universal Law and his list of obligatory ends in the *Metaphysik der Sitten* is that he did not argue that seeking others' happiness in general was a duty, but only that helping at least some of them when in need was a duty. But a simple generalization of the argument showing help to some of those in need a duty can be used to show the promotion of at least some others' happiness in other ways also a duty. Consider the incomplete maxim of ends:

6. I will neglect everything needed to promote any other's happiness.

Its UTC is:

7. Everybody will neglect everything needed to promote any other's happiness.

If I will 7, then I also will that everybody neglect everything needed to promote my own happiness. But as an agent with ends, I by definition desire my own happiness, i.e., the realization of my various ends. And as a rational agent who intends some means to whatever ends he has, I intend whatever is needed to promote my own happiness. If another's acts are necessary for my happiness I intend that he do those acts. So I cannot consistently intend that others neglect everything needed for my happiness.

This argument shows the promotion of others' happiness to be a duty in rather a limited sense only. Agents are bound only to do some of what is essential if some other's happiness is not to be thwarted; they are not bound to do everything needed for any one person's happiness, or even to make some contribution toward everybody's happiness. But even this limited duty of promoting others' happiness requires a great deal, though falling far short of the fantastic demands often imputed to Kantian duties.

If it is a duty to pursue one's own moral and natural perfection and the happiness of others, why is it not a duty to pursue also one's own happiness and others' moral and natural perfection? Surely the Formula of Universal Law requires us not to make distinctions between ourselves and others? But Kant does not think that he is making groundless distinctions. It is true that a maxim of neglecting our own happiness could be shown inconsistent with the duty to promote others' happiness. An agent who intended such neglect and also intended others to neglect his happiness would be intending others to violate their duty. But there are no such agents. Since any agent who has ends desires his own happiness, no agent could rationally have a maxim of neglecting his own happiness. Hence, one's own happiness is no duty, for we do not have to be constrained to its pursuit. It is a necessary end of creatures with ends, and for that very reason not an obligatory end.[44]

A second argument shows why others' perfection cannot be an obligatory end. Perfection consists in our own capacity to do certain acts and to adopt certain ends. Others cannot make us perfect. So the natural and moral perfection of others cannot be an obligatory end since it is an impossible one. Obligatory ends must be neither impossible nor necessary, and are thus restricted to those ends which fall under the general headings of our own perfection and others' happiness.[45]

[44] *M.S.*, p. 385.

[45] Kant does admit that this argument is too sweeping, for we can do some things to promote others' perfection. We can at any rate preserve them from temptation, and we can do something about their moral education. We can do rather more to educate their natural talents, cf. *M.S.*, p. 393, and also the "Ethical Doctrine of Method," *M.S.*, p. 476. But he is inclined to shove any such duties under the heading of promoting others' happiness, and specifically their "moral well-being." At this point the architectonic of the doctrine of virtue creaks.

If we apply that Formula of Universal Law to maxims of ends as well as to maxims of action, it is not difficult to justify the two obligatory ends under which Kant arranges all duties of virtue in the *Metaphysik der Sitten*. When testing maxims of ends, the contradiction in the will test uses in a rather different way two premises also used by the contradiction in conception test. It assumes that men have ends (indeed this is presupposed in the very application of a test to maxims of ends) and that it is irrational not to intend some sufficient means to an end which is aimed at, i.e., the Principle of Hypothetical Imperatives. On the other hand, the contradiction in the will test makes less use of the principle that we must intend the normal and predictable results of acts we intend.

What can the contradiction in the will test do beyond establishing those obligatory ends already considered? Are there obligatory ends which Kant fails to consider in the *Tugendlehre?* What must be added to the test to show that the subsidiary duties which he does consider in the *Tugendlehre* are duties of virtue? The next chapter will consider what further obligatory ends there may be; here I shall try to sketch the test for subsidiary duties of virtue in the light of the distinctions made in chapter 4 between ethical duties of omission and ethical duties of commission.

Ethical duties of omission are duties to refrain from acts or patterns of action that would make it impossible to achieve some obligatory end. So, given that we know which ends are obligatory, it is a matter for empirical judgment to work out which acts and omissions are required by virtue. We have only to test an agent's *complete* maxim of ends, assuming that his end is not to prevent his own perfection or others' happiness. Refraining from suicide is a duty, not for the reasons Kant gave when he tried to classify it as a duty of justice, but because destruction of the material conditions for human action is incompatible with pursuit of any obligatory ends. Drunkenness is contrary to virtue because it incapacitates the agent from any action, including therefore pursuit of obligatory ends. Similarly of duties of respect to others: by mocking and derision we make the pursuit of virtue harder.

There is room for much argument about the list of ethical duties of omission with which Kant is finally content. Some of his list may seem to make duties of trivial omissions; and perhaps there are other omissions which are crucial if obligatory ends are to be pursued. There may even be duties of wide obligation but narrow requirement which demand specific performances rather than specific omissions. All these matters can be investigated; but in each case the pattern of argument would be simple: it would depend on ascertaining what conditions are necessary in a given situation if the obligatory ends are to be pursued. These are matters for casuistry, which Kant recognizes as an entirely legitimate part of ethical argument, though not one which has any part in a metaphysic of morals.[46]

The argument pattern for determining which are the ethical duties of commission is rather different. Ethical duties of commission are wide both in obligation and in requirement. They are duties to adopt certain policies falling under the very general policies of pursuing our own perfection and others' happiness. The simplest way for verifying whether the adoption of any policy is an ethical duty of commission is to see whether the end to be aimed at is a part of the end of promoting others' happiness or our own perfection. Thus, not harming others is plausibly part of promoting their happiness and maintaining our health is plausibly part of promoting our own perfection. A more formal way of checking which ends are required by ethical duties of commission is to apply the contradiction in the will test directly to each end. We can, for instance, ask of a maxim of neglecting to show gratitude whether it would pass the contradition in the will test. If it were to do so, we would have to be able to intend its UTC,

8. Everyone will neglect everything needed to show gratitude for favors received.

If we intend 8, we intend also that others tend to show us no gratitude as well as the normal and predictable results of the lack of gratitude holding as a law of nature: that favors become less frequent. If we intend this, we intend also that we be less likely to receive favors; and this is incompatible with intending that anything needed for the realization of whatever ends we may have be done. Again there may be room for dispute about Kant's actual list of ethical duties of commission, but the methods casuistry may use to resolve such disputes are clear.

The contradiction in the will test, like the contradiction in conception test, is an effective test under an interpretation which has strong textual support; its conclusions are by and large plausible, and agree fairly closely with Kant's claims.

[46] *M.S.*, p. 410.

CHAPTER SIX

AN ASSESSMENT
OF KANT'S ETHICAL THEORY

The interpretation of the Categorical Imperative presented in the last two chapters shows that Kant's ethical theory can effectively classify acts under two headings. It can determine whether they are obligatory, merely permissible, or forbidden, and whether they are morally worthy, lacking in moral worth, or morally unworthy. Kant, it seems, has both a theory of right action and a theory of morally worthy action.

On closer inspection this impression becomes less definite. Are the moral categories which Kant's theory discriminates in fact those which his labels suggest? Do they correspond to the moral categories distinguished either in common speech or by other theorists? Has he provided decision procedures for either the rightness (i.e., obligatoriness and mere permissibility) or the moral worth of acts in the senses in which we normally use those terms? To answer these questions we must step back from the Kantian texts.

I Kant and Supererogation

The first step back brings into focus Kant's basic ethical categories and their logical relations. Kant's account of the basic categories of ethics has recently been challenged by Eisenberg,[1] who contends that Kant's theory of right and morally worthy action is seriously incomplete because he cannot allow for acts of supererogation, and has to misclassify such acts as fulfillments of duties. I shall consider this charge against Kant's theory before moving on to the charges often brought that more global defects mar the theory.

[1] P. Eisenberg, p. 267.

Eisenberg accepts that Kant has a theory of right, since he distinguishes obligatory, merely permissible, and forbidden acts. Unlike some other Kantian commentators to whom he refers,[2] he thinks that Kant can also allow for acts which are not only merely permissible but also morally indifferent, i.e., of no moral concern at all, and for acts which are merely permissible and yet offensive, i.e., which it is bad to do. But he denies that Kant can allow for supererogatory acts, permissible acts which it is good to do.[3]

At various points in his article Eisenberg describes his project in different ways. Initially he claims to be investigating "the number of basic ethical categories . . . that Kant takes account of or allows for." [4] But he concludes the article by claiming that Kant cannot "give adequate recognition" to the category of supererogatory acts.[5] There is a gap between these two descriptions. The fact that supererogation is not among Kant's *basic* categories is in itself no reason for thinking that he cannot allow for supererogatory acts. In fact, Eisenberg starts, not with Kant's basic ethical concepts, but from a list of his own that coincides only in part with Kant's.

Both lists of ethical concepts allow for the three deontic or 'legal' concepts. Whereas Kant distinguishes in addition to these the morally worthy, the lacking in moral worth, and the morally unworthy, Eisenberg's other categories are the supererogatory, the morally indifferent, and the offensive. The curious thing about Eisenberg's nondeontic categories is that none of them is "basic" in the sense of being primitive, for they cannot be defined independently of one or another (it does not matter which) of the deontic categories. By contrast Kant's three nondeontic categories seem to be defined independently of his deontic categories.[6] Further, while Eisenberg's "basic" categories define a single set of mutually exclusive and jointly exhaustive categories into one and only one of which any act must fall, Kant's basic categories define two such sets, and any act must fall into one and only one category in each set.

Theoretically, then, Kant can allow for an act's having any one of nine derivative statuses, since this is the number of possible combinations of deontic and ethical status. The ones which he in fact allows for can be seen in Table 4.2. In that table there are classes of acts which are obligatory and

[2] R. Chisholm, "Supererogation and Offense," *Ratio*, Vol. 5, 1963; J. O. Urmson, "Saints and Heroes," in *Essays in Moral Philosophy*, ed. A. I. Melden.
[3] For Eisenberg's definitions see P. Eisenberg, p. 256.   [4] *Ibid.*, p. 255.
[5] *Ibid.*, p. 269.   [6] See section III for discussion of this problem.

morally worthy, and of acts which are merely permissible and morally worthy. Acts which are obligatory and morally worthy are principled performances of duties of justice and of ethical duties of omission. Acts which are merely permissible and morally worthy are some implementations of ethical duties of commission, i.e., of duties to adopt certain maxims of ends. Should either of these sets of acts be called supererogatory?

If one defines supererogatory acts as those which go beyond duty in the sense of doing *more* than is obligatory, then it would seem that acts which are obligatory and also morally worthy are acts of supererogation. If, on the other hand, like Eisenberg, one defines supererogatory acts as acts which though not obligatory are morally worthy, then Kant also can allow for these.[7] The main objection to either of these definitions comes simply from an etymological perspective on the meaning of "supererogatory." Eisenberg points out that Kant speaks of all morally worthy acts as acts of duty, while by supererogatory acts we mean those that are beyond duty. But we need not conclude that Kant is committing "the error of treating as duties certain things which are properly classed as supererogatory." [8] The term "duty" does not have either in common usage or in ethical theory so definite or so restricted a sense—as Eisenberg's subsequent discussions of other theorists who have classified supererogatory acts as (some sort of) duty shows. It is not a clearcut mistake each time a person characterizes an act of supererogation as "only doing my duty" or as something he ought to do. The important thing is that Kant allows for acts which are meritorious in a certain way without being obligatory. That he calls such acts duties is relatively trivial.

On the other hand, Eisenberg's claim that Kant can allow for morally indifferent and for offensive acts can be sustained by referring to the table on page 56, though Kant's definitions of these concepts do not entirely tally with Eisenberg's. Kant does not use the notions of a good or bad act as fundamental categories, but rather the notion of a morally worthy or unworthy act. Whether this has any important bearing on his theory we must now determine. Certainly it has been claimed that it does. For Kant's list of ethical concepts has often been held to reveal a far more serious defect about his theory's views on the relation between rightness and goodness than its alleged incapacity to take account of acts of supererogation.

[7] Cf. T. E. Hill, p. 73.   [8] P. Eisenberg, p. 267.

✲✲✲ II The Right and the Good in Kant's Ethical Theory

The most serious and recurrent criticism made of Kant's list of ethical categories was put forward by Prichard in these words:

Kant's main mistake does not lie in his account of moral goodness [i.e., of moral worth] . . . [but] in representing moral goodness as the basis of duty [i.e., of obligatory action]. The truth is that Kant is here guilty of an inversion. Whereas, in fact, to arrive at the idea that certain acts are morally good, we must already, and so independently, have the idea that there are acts which are duties, Kant is maintaining that to arrive at the latter idea we must already, and so independently, have the former.[9]

In this passage Prichard is claiming that Kant makes the morally good or worthy prior to the obligatory, and by so doing makes his whole ethical theory incoherent, for no account of moral worth can be given which does not depend on the notion of obligation. We shall have to see whether Prichard is correct in each of these claims. Is it true that Kant makes moral worth prior to obligation? Is it true that obligation is in fact prior to moral worth?

Prichard's argument has been stated in a more precise version by Ross.[10] He maintains that Kant holds that the motive from which we ought to act when we do an act of duty is the sense of duty, and so that any statement of the form "It is my duty to do act A from the sense of duty" should be expandable into a statement of the form "It is my duty to do act A from the sense that it is my duty to do act A." Since the second part of statements of the latter form should be similarly expandable, we are led into an infinite regress. This argument makes use of only one of Prichard's two premises. It assumes that Kant does make moral worth prior to obligation, and shows how this assumption leads to trouble. It is a corollary, and not a premise, of this argument that moral worth cannot be prior to obligation, and not even a corollary of the argument that obligation must be prior to moral worth—for the two concepts might be interdependent, or unconnected.

[9] H. A. Prichard, "Moral Obligation," p. 156, and see also his "Does Moral Philosophy Rest on a Mistake?" especially pp. 7, 13. Both essays are in *Moral Obligation*.
[10] D. Ross, *The Right and the Good*, p. 5.

Is this, in fact, a fair representation of Kant's position? Does he make moral worth prior to obligation? If he does so, does it have the devastating consequences which both Prichard and Ross suggest? The sort of morally worthy acts which these writers have in mind are morally worthy performances of duties of justice, which, like other morally worthy acts, must be done for certain motives or ends. But their objections would apply equally to morally worthy performances of ethical duties of omission. In all such cases we must assess a complete maxim of ends, rendered schematically by

(4) To − − − − if · · · · in order to ──── .

The problem is the filling of the final "────." What is the purposive component of maxims on which acts which are both obligatory and morally worthy are done? If we fill in "────" simply by some reference to the pure, moral motive the result is unilluminating. We find ourselves contemplating formulas which end with some such phrase as "to do my duty" or "to show reverence for the law."

Ross is quite right in contending that some reference must be made in the purposive component to the act description of the maxim of action. That act description, *ex hypothesi,* describes an obligatory act. If reference is to be made to the act in the purposive component of maxims fitting schema (4), then it seems that we have a maxim of doing some duty for the sake of duty. Let us therefore consider a maxim of the form:

(4′) To − − − − if · · · · in order to − − − − if · · · ·

An instance of a maxim of form (4′) would be:

To refrain from stealing if tempted in order to refrain from stealing if tempted.

But this is not quite what we want. Obstinate but unreasoned honesty is not morally worthy. Reverence for the law is not a blind refusal to act for further reasons. If an agent's act is to be done out of reverence for the law, he must realize that his maxim of action is a maxim of duty, and act in order to do his duty. In the phrase "reverence for the law," the term "law" is a variable, ranging over all practical laws, i.e., over all practical principles whose form is that required by the moral law. Reverence for the law is not reverence for the particular law that has been adopted as a maxim of action. So the maxim we must act on to do a just and morally worthy act must fit, not schema (4′), but the more exacting schema (8).

(8) To − − − − if · · · in order to carry out my duty to − − − − if · · · ·

Maxims of this form seem to be open to precisely the infinite regress that Ross pointed out. To the purposive component of a complete maxim of ends, one can always add a purposive component. But there is no reason to do so, and good reason not to do so.

The reason that Ross's *reductio* of Kant's position seems plausible is that he schematizes Kant's position on the assumption that doing some act, A, and doing it from a certain motive can be duties in precisely the same sense. His rendering of Kant's position can be schematized:

A. It is my duty to do act A from the sense that it is my duty to do act A.

Here the second occurrence of the term "duty," like the first, is taken to refer both to the act A and to the motive with which it must be done. This is what licenses embarkation on the infinite regress. But if we rewrite Ross's schema to make this assumption explicit, we get

B. It is obligatory for me to do act A from the sense that it is obligatory for me to do act A.

And B is not a fair rendering of Kant's position. If it is obligatory for me to do act A, this means that A is a duty of justice or an ethical duty of omission. The argument pattern to show these acts obligatory cannot be extended to show that their performance with certain motives is obligatory. The initial "It is obligatory for. . . ." must have its scope restricted to exclude the purposive component. B must be replaced by:

C. It is obligatory for me to do act A and morally worthy for me to do so from the sense that it is obligatory for me to do so.

Maxims which fit schema (8) are compatible with this assignment of statuses, and C is not subject to any infinite regress such as Ross' assignment of moral statuses leads one into. Schema (8) exhibits the form which an agent's complete maxim of ends must have if he is to carry out an obligation in a morally worthy way. Ross has not shown that the relationship which Kant holds exists between the obligatory and the morally worthy leads him into any difficulty. Ross's argument is based on a failure to distinguish two sorts of duty which Kant does distinguish. We have, however, yet to see the relationship between obligation and moral worth in Kant's theory.

Recently Kant has been commended for holding the view which both Ross and Prichard denied he could hold. Grice quotes:

The concept of good and evil must not be determined before the moral law (of which it seems it must be the foundation), but only after it and by means of it.[11]

He interprets this as meaning that Kant makes obligation prior to moral worth:

It seems . . . that judgments of moral good are logically prior to judgments of what ought to be done. The converse is the truth: the structure of morals can be made intelligible only if the grounds of judgments of obligation are set out first, so that the discharge of obligations can be referred to in the grounds of judgments of moral good.[12]

In the section of the *Kritik der Praktischen Vernunft* from which Grice quotes, Kant's main concern is to distinguish the good in the sense of the useful or pleasant from the morally good and to explicate the latter concept. If ethics could be heteronomous, if it could be based on human desires or preferences, then the good in the sense of the useful or pleasant might be prior to obligation. This is the assumption of utilitarian ethical theories. But since ethics cannot be heteronomous, we cannot form a determinate concept of the morally good without referring to the moral law. The only concept of a good object which is compatible with the will's not being determined by an object of desire (i.e., heteronomously) is the indeterminate concept of an

---

[11] *K.P.V.*, p. 63, but quoted from Abbott's translation, p. 154.

[12] R. Grice, *The Grounds of Moral Judgement,* p. 177. Cf. also p. 7. He there assigns to Prichard the contrary view, i.e. that good is prior to right. This looks confusing, but is correct in that Prichard thought good prior to right, but right prior to morally worthy action.

object (whatever it may be) "suitable to determine the will *a priori.*" Hence, the moral law is prior to the morally good, for it is the moral law which alone can determine the will *a priori.* We must not be misled by the first part of the *Grundlegung* where it seems as though Kant takes the concept of a good will as the fundamental ethical concept. This is done only to show that the concept of a good will cannot be explicated except in terms of the moral law.

The moral law, as formulated in the various statements of the Categorical Imperative, is the fundamental ethical principle; and in ethics principles are prior to concepts. The moral law is prior to the notion of a morally good or worthy act, and that is the only concept of good which has any place in ethics:

> Had one previously analyzed the practical law, he would have found . . . not that the concept of the good as an object of the moral law determines the latter and makes it possible, but rather the reverse, i.e. that the moral law is that which first defines the concept of the good—so far as it absolutely deserves this name—and makes it possible.[13]

But to say that the moral law determines what is morally good is not to say that the concept of an obligatory act is prior to that of a morally good or worthy act. Both concepts are dependent in complex ways on the moral law, but not identical with it. So this passage of the *Kritik der Praktischen Vernunft* does not show that Kant thinks obligation prior to moral goodness or worth. Neither of the arguments we have examined has shown that one branch of Kant's ethical theory is prior to the other.

𝒜𝓀 III Obligation and Moral Worth

The reason for trying to settle the priority between Kant's theory of obligation and his theory of moral worth is that an answer will be useful for assessing the adequacy of his entire ethical theory. If one branch of the theory is wholly dependent on the other, difficulties in one area may infect the whole theory. Only if the two parts of this ethical theory are independent of one another, or only partially dependent, may defects be confined to one part of the theory.

[13] *K.P.V.,* p. 66.

On the basis of the interpretation in the last chapter we can draw up two preliminary definitions.

A. Obligatory acts and omissions are those the contrary of whose maxim of action does not meet the requirements of the moral law, and those which are required in all circumstances by some policy the contrary of whose maxim of ends does not meet the requirements of the moral law.

The two parts of this definition cover, respectively, those obligatory acts required by justice and those required by ethical duties of omission. The second preliminary definition reads:

B. Morally worthy acts and omissions are those obligatory acts and omissions which are done in order to do obligatory acts and omissions, and those acts and omissions the contrary of whose maxims of ends do not meet the requirements of the moral law.

The two parts of this definition cover, respectively, those morally worthy acts and omissions which are performances of duties of justice from a "pure" or "moral" motive and those morally worthy acts and omissions which are fulfillments of duties of virtue.

These preliminary definitions seem to show that neither obligation nor moral worth can be prior in Kant's ethical theory. Some morally worthy acts and omissions are defined in terms of obligatory acts and omissions, and some obligatory acts and omissions are defined in terms of the ends which make acts morally worthy.

But before we conclude the two branches of Kant's ethical theory are interdependent, it is necessary to examine his theory of moral worth more closely. That theory seems to have two distinct incarnations. In the *Grundlegung,* morally worthy acts are usually defined in terms of the motive from which they are done. Such acts must be done from "reverence for the law" or from "the sense of duty." On the other hand, in the *Metaphysik der Sitten,* morally worthy action is defined in terms of the obligatory ends at which it aims. The previous chapter concentrated on the latter approach to moral worth, while claiming that the duality was, in fact, illusory since Kant's theory of ends and his theory of motives were two sides of one coin. The time has now come to make good these claims. If motives and ends are so closely connected, it may be possible to simplify definition B and define moral worth either entirely in terms of motives or entirely in terms of ends.

Let us begin with the theory of motives of the *Grundlegung*. Kant there distinguishes various sorts of motives: interests and inclinations (all empirical motives), and one pure motive, reverence for the law.[14] In stating an agent's maxim of ends, the purposive component must be filled out with a reference to the agent's end. But this part of the maxim can always also be interpreted as referring to the agent's motive. If a man's maxim of ends is "To harm my former employer to retaliate for my dismissal," the purposive component can be read as referring either to the agent's end or to his motive. Revenge is both his motive and his end.

All empirical motives are impulsions to achieve some desired end. These motives can all be classified as *self-love*. Under this heading fall many common, and less common, motives such as revenge, gratitude, selfishness, affection, spite, *Schadenfreude*, and so on. These species of self-love are differentiated from one another by their object or end. But all their ends can be classified under the heading of *happiness*. Self-love in general aims at the agent's happiness. "Happiness" is just a generic term by which indeterminate reference can be made to all the particular ends an agent desires. Just as self-love is not a separate motive with its own peculiar object, but the form of all motives that point to an end desired, so happiness is not a separate end but the form of all ends an agent may desire. The connection between motives and ends is logical. If an agent desires some state of affairs, x, we may attribute to him either the motive "desire for x" (which may in some cases have a more compendious name, enshrined in a "case term")[15] or state that x is one of his ends.

Can this connection between empirical motives and subjective ends be used to illuminate the connection between the pure, moral motive and objective ends? If it can, we may be able to elucidate further phrases such as "reverence for the law" and "sense of duty." If it cannot, these terms will remain

[14] Kant's terminology is not particularly consistent. At *G.*, p. 427, he reserves the term "motive" (*Bewegungsgrund*) for the one moral motive, and calls any empirical motive an impulsion (*Triebfeder*). By contrast, in *K.P.V.*, pp. 74–92, he uses the latter term as the generic one. However, he always marks the same distinction whatever his terminology. For a discussion of the implications of these switches in terminology for Kant's theory of action see L. W. Beck, *A Commentary on Kant's Critique of Practical Reason*, p. 214.

[15] For this terminology, see E. D'Arcy, *Human Acts*, pp. 21–24 and below, pp. 141–42.

an idle and mysterious part of Kant's ethical theory, serving only to raise puzzles about what he means by calling a motive pure and what the psychological status of such motives can be.

Let us return to the *Grundlegung*. There Kant characterizes morally worthy action in terms of its motive. A cursory reading might suggest that he thinks acts which are just and morally worthy must be done for no end at all. But this is clearly incompatible with his view that all action has some end. In the previous chapter I argued that there is no reason within Kant's writings for thinking that all ends must be ends desired and that it is quite consistent for him to apply the Categorical Imperative to maxims of ends. Now something more positive must be said about those ends which are not or not merely ends desired. We have the advantage of being able to approach the problem either via the notion of a pure motive or more directly by considering Kant's theory of objective ends.

In the *Grundlegung* those who act from pure motive act with the end of instantiating the moral law in their action. Their complete maxim of ends fits schema (8) of the previous section. It has the form "To − − − − if · · · · in order to do my duty to − − − − if · · · ·" To act from reverence for the law is to act on maxims because they meet the requirements of the Categorical Imperative:

Nothing but the idea of law . . . so far as it . . . is the ground determining the will can constitute that preeminent good which we call moral, a good which is already present in the person acting on this idea and has not to be awaited merely from the result.[16]

To have the sort of intentions that meet this description is to have what Kant calls a good will. The end of morally worthy action, according to the first part of the *Grundlegung*, is the good will exemplified in such action. If an agent does a morally worthy act we can attribute to him both a specific motive and a specific end. The end is that of exemplifying a will determined by the requirements of the moral law; the motive is that of doing what the moral law requires. Like empirical motives, the pure motive is logically connected to a certain sort of end.

But though we have now recast the account of morally worthy action of the first part of the *Grundlegung* so that it refers to ends, we have still to consider the doctrine of obligatory ends of the *Metaphysik der Sitten*. There Kant

[16] *G.,* p. 401.

appears to dispense with any account of morally worthy action in terms of motives, and to rely exclusively on the notion of an obligatory end in his account of morally worthy action. And the obligatory ends of the latter work do not seem to bear any very close resemblance to the good will. Indeed the term "obligatory end" is never used in the *Grundlegung* to refer to the good will. The good will is said to be a good-in-itself and a self-existent end [17]— but never an obligatory end. The task of reconciling the two accounts of morally worthy action has not been simplified very much by looking at the *Grundlegung* account in terms of ends rather than of motives.

When we look more closely at the texts, the problem turns out to require more than a reconciliation of the *Grundlegung* and the *Metaphysik der Sitten*. Within the former work Kant singles out certain ends other than a good will as *ends in themselves* and *objective ends*. Rational natures are such ends, and so, in particular, are human natures.[18] We are therefore faced with trying to see the connections between the good will, rational and therefore human nature, and the two obligatory ends, the happiness of others and one's own perfection.

As a preliminary simplification we can see why Kant refers to the former two as self-existent or objective ends or as ends in themselves and to the latter two as obligatory ends. The difference of terminology is a reflection of the fact that the *Grundlegung* discusses practical laws which hold for rational agents in general, while the *Metaphysik der Sitten* is concerned with the duties of men. The concept of obligation, like that of duty, has no application to wholly rational natures. Obligations imply constraint of desires. No end can be obligatory for rational natures in general, any more than acts can be obligatory for them. On the other hand, there can be ends that are objective for rational nature in general, just as there are objective moral laws governing action. For the sake of clarity, I shall refer to all those ends that Kant calls "ends in themselves," "obligatory ends," "self-existent ends," "ends which it is a duty to have," and so on as "objective ends," remembering that any objective end is an obligatory end for agents who are, like men, not wholly rational.

With this preliminary aside, we return to the question of the connections between the various objective ends which Kant lists. The problem is one of the more complex and baffling in Kantian interpretation. Any investigation of objective ends, of the "ends of pure practical reason," leads easily into an

[17] *G.*, pp. 394, 396 and 437.   [18] *G.*, pp. 427–29.

investigation of their systematic union, i.e., of the entire object of pure practical reason that Kant calls the *summum bonum*. A consideration of the *summum bonum* can hardly avoid investigating the postulates Kant thinks are needed to make that notion coherent. And so by easy steps one can be led into an examination of Kant's views on God, freedom, and immortality. But a more modest approach is all that is needed. The aim, after all, is only to determine the relation between moral worth and obligation in Kant's ethical theory.

The immediate problem can be stated very simply: If morally worthy acts are those done for the sake of the moral law, why should acts done to treat other rational natures as ends, to perfect ourselves, or to make others happy be considered morally worthy? Why should one suppose that acts done for these ends are done with the moral motive? Why should there be more than one objective end—the good will—corresponding to the single moral motive?

Unfortunately Kant does not set out systematically the connections which he thinks hold between the various objective ends. In the *Metaphysik der Sitten* he provides a couple of interesting, if sketchy, arguments to show that there must be at least one objective end.[19] He claims that if there is even one objective end, then this must by the previous argument be the good will. I shall try to go beyond this and argue that if there is one objective end—the good will—then there are also those other objective ends which Kant lists. Kant himself does not show systematically why these ends must be just the ones he lists. But the following picture—I do not claim that it is in all respects a satisfying argument—fills in what he suggests.

The claim that rational nature exists as an end in itself, an objective end, is introduced without argument.[20] But later Kant does argue that rational nature is such an end because a good will is an objective end. It is because rational nature is the only possessor of a will which can be good that rational nature is an end in itself.[21] If good willing is an end which it is a duty to have, then the maintenance and cultivation or promotion of rational natures, at least in those respects that are necessary or helpful for them to have good wills, is also an end which it is a duty to have. If we must intend some sufficient means to any end we intend, and good willing is such an end, then we must also intend the maintenance and cultivation of rational natures. So

[19] *M.S.,* pp. 383, 394.   [20] *G.,* pp. 427–29.   [21] *G.,* p. 437.

rational, and in particular human, nature is an objective end.[22] We can argue from the claim that the good will is an objective end to the Formula of the End in Itself.

But what exactly should we understand by the preservation and cultivation of (human) rational nature? In his examples of what must be done to treat men as ends and never as mere means, Kant interprets the maintenance of human nature as avoiding the destruction of its animal substratum and not impeding rational natures in their pursuit of ends, and the cultivation and promotion of rational nature as the development of human talents and providing positive help to rational natures in their pursuit of ends, i.e., in their quest for happiness.[23]

Clearly he sees a close connection between maintaining human rational nature and the ethical duties of omission, and between promoting human rational nature and the ethical duties of commission. But how can one show more convincingly that not treating men as means involves doing nothing to prevent human perfection and happiness, while treating them as ends involves doing some of what is needed to promote human perfection and happiness?

One discrepancy at least can be removed. The Formula of the End in Itself requires us to treat all men—ourselves and others—as ends and not as mere means. But the doctrine of obligatory ends of the *Metaphysik der Sitten* seems to require differential treatment; we are to preserve and promote, not happiness and perfection in general, but our own perfection and others' happiness. In this case Kant does give explicit arguments to explain the restrictions on the doctrine of obligatory ends.[24] Our own happiness cannot be an obligatory end because each man necessarily desires his own happiness (whatever he desires is by definition his happiness) while the notion of obligation or duty implies some constraint on the pursuit of ends desired by finitely rational wills.[25] The perfection of others cannot be an obligatory end because it is not a possible end: perfection must be cultivated by each man for himself. (I have already remarked that this seems to be true only of moral perfection.)

---

[22] There are, of course, epistemological difficulties in Kant's claim that we can know other humans to be rational natures in the strong sense which Kant's theory of freedom requires. This topic is discussed by P. Haezrahi, "The Concept of Man as End-in-Himself," *Kant-Studien,* Vol. 53, 1962, and by R. P. Wolff, *The Autonomy of Reason,* pp. 9–24.

[23] *G.,* pp. 429–30.   [24] *M.S.,* pp. 384–85, and cf. above p. 91.

[25] *Gl,* pp. 414, 439; *M.S.,* p. 221.

The gap between the scope of the Formula of the End in Itself and the doctrine of obligatory ends, is, like the two phrases themselves, a reflection of the fact that the *Grundlegung* is concerned with the moral requirements on rational beings as such and the *Metaphysik der Sitten* with the moral requirements on men, whose desire for happiness and limited capacity to perfect one another place certain limitations on the ends which it can be a duty for them to have.

I return to Kant's reasons for thinking that treating rational nature as an end in itself under the limitations of human life amounts to having the policies of perfecting oneself and making others happy. For once Kant provides one of the very arguments required. He argues directly from the Formula of the End in Itself to the duty of perfecting oneself:

The power to set an end—any end whatsoever—is the characteristic of humanity (as distinguished from animality). Hence there is also bound up with the end of humanity in our own person the rational will, and so the duty, to make ourselves worthy of humanity by culture in general, by pursuing or promoting the *power* to realize all possible ends, so far as this power is to be found in man himself.[26]

This argument is not very clear, and there is no companion argument leading from the Formula of the End in Itself to the duty to preserve and promote others' happiness. Kant, in fact, uses the Formula of Universal Law to show that others' happiness is an objective end.[27] Rather than try to provide a detailed interpretation of the passage just quoted, I shall put forward an argument which travels from the same starting point to the same conclusion, and then on to the conclusion that others' happiness is an objective end.

In saying that the power to set ends is characteristic of humanity, Kant means that only a being who exercises this power can be held to act rationally. Other creatures—animals, Kant says, but it may be true of machines also—may produce results or pursue in more or less intelligent ways objectives which instinct, preference, or a program have given them. But the hallmark of rational action is the capacity to choose among ends. Rational beings can choose between maxims of ends; they can even choose to neglect subjective ends.

We have already established that if good willing is an end in itself or objective end, then so are rational beings. We can now go one step further: If

[26] *M.S.*, p. 391.   [27] Cf. *M.S.*, p. 312.

rational beings are objective ends, then so is their capacity to set ends. This capacity is an essential part of any rational being, without which such a being could not have a good will. Further, if rational beings are actually to pursue objective ends, then they not only need the capacity to set ends, but also must use this capacity to select objective ends. If the existence of good willing is an objective end, so is the pursuit of objective ends by rational beings. Good willing cannot arise in any other way. To intend that there be good willing and some sufficient set of means for this end to be realized requires one to intend that rational beings exercise their capacity to select ends by selecting objective ends.

If it is an objective end that rational beings—ourselves and others—select objective ends, then any subsidiary end needed to ensure that they do so is also an objective end. There are two such subsidiary ends. First, if rational beings lack the talents and abilities needed to pursue whatever ends they may be required to pursue, they may under some circumstances be unable to pursue any end, including objective ends. So it is an objective end to cultivate the capacity to pursue ends. Given the varied circumstances of human life, this means that some natural talents and abilities and the one moral talent—strength of will—must be objective ends.

The principle used in moving from the premise that the exercise of a capacity to set objective ends is an objective end to the conclusion that our own perfection is an objective end is once again the Principle of Hypothetical Imperatives: we must intend some set of means sufficient for any end intended. Since the pursuit of objective ends in human life may demand many skills and abilities, and will always require moral strength, we must do whatever is possible (much in our own case, little or nothing in the case of others) to develop various skills and abilities and moral strength.

Second, from the premise that the pursuit of objective ends by all rational beings is an objective end, we can argue on very similar lines that the happiness of others is an objective end. By the Principle of Hypothetical Imperatives, if we make the pursuit of objective ends our end, we must intend some sufficient set of means for its realization. In the varied circumstances of human life, the development of sundry talents and of moral strength will not prove a sufficient means to this end. Men will often need the help and cooperation of others in their pursuit of ends, including their pursuit of objective ends. There is no way to tell *a priori* just what sort of help or cooperation may be needed. So the only description we can give of the objective end we must adopt is that of sharing others' objective ends. But since we cannot easily tell whether others' ends are objective, any more than we can be sure about our own ends, the need for sharing others' ends cannot be restricted to those cases where it is *known* that they are pursuing objective ends. Rather we must share their ends unless they are forbidden. But if we do this, then we have made their happiness, except in those cases where they desire something forbidden, an end. If the pursuit of objective ends is an objective end, then so must be the happiness of others.

I have now sketched connections between all the objective ends which Kant discusses. There remains the question of whether there may not be ends other than our own perfection and others' happiness which are obligatory for partially rational natures. I shall not try to answer this question. The exact scope of the ends of promoting one's own perfection and others' happiness is not at all precisely determined by the sorts of arguments presented in this section, so it seems likely that it would be very hard to show whether there are or are not any further obligatory ends.[28]

This sketch of Kant's theory of ends has shown a means by which the doctrine of the pure motive can be interpreted in terms of certain conditions on the purposive components of the complete maxims of ends of morally worthy acts, and how the resulting account of the most general objective end, the good will, can be connected, without reliance on the Formula of Universal Law, to the doctrine of rational nature as an end in itself and the doctrine of human obligatory ends.

This excursion has shown that the connection and elaboration of Kant's theory of motives and ends makes it possible to state a second and simpler definition of morally worthy action and omission, a definition not dependent on the notion of an obligatory act. We can define all morally worthy action in terms of the end at which it aims:

B′. Morally worthy acts and omissions are those which are done on a maxim
of ends whose contrary does not meet the requirements of the moral law.

---

[28] One suggestion for determining them more precisely would be to try to derive the principle of comparative advantage from the conjunction of the two human obligatory ends. The talents which we must develop are those which will be most useful to us in contributing to the ends of others. Since this holds for everyone, each can rely on others, so need not develop all his talents. Rather he should in all cases try to acquire those skills with which he could help others and at which he may expect to be relatively better, but should omit to acquire those skills with which he might help others, but at which he can expect to be relatively worse. Each person therefore develops his best talents regardless of how his best compares to others' best.

Whether we are aiming at a good will, at the preservation and promotion of rational nature, or more narrowly at perfecting ouselves or making others happy, our end is objective, and for men obligatory. For an act to be morally worthy it is not necessary or sufficient that it *result* in the promotion of an objective end. The objective end must be aimed for, but it need not be realized. Morally worthy acts need only strive for objective ends in the knowledge that they are such ends. Provided the purposive component of an agent's maxim meets these conditions, he is acting "for the sake of duty." The moral motive aims at any of the objective ends.

To act "out of reverence for the law" or "from a sense of duty" is to pursue ends of the sort which have just been discussed. It is not to act with any peculiar feeling of reverence or awe. It may be that morally worthy action is accompanied by or induces such feelings. But Kant's test of the moral worth of acts does not assume that we assess agents' feelings. Pathology, as Kant would have it—psychology, as we would say—is irrelevant to the moral worth of acts. To determine an agent's motive is to determine his purpose in acting. Whatever he feels about this purpose—joy or reluctance, enthusiasm or misgivings, respect or contempt—his act has moral worth if and only if his purpose falls under one of the objective ends whose systematic interconnection has just been sketched.

Definition B' shows that once we have assimilated Kant's theory of ends it is possible to give a definition of moral worth not dependent on the notion of obligatory action. Moral worth is not a dependent notion in Kant's ethical theory.

But it seems that no similar independent definition of obligatory action can be given. The obligatoriness of some actions is derivative from the obligatoriness of certain ends, and the truth of certain means/ends statements. But this is true only of those obligations which are ethical duties of omission. It would, therefore, be wrong to say that Kant's account of obligation is dependent on his account of moral worth, and more accurate to say that he has two separate accounts of obligation, the less important being dependent on his account of moral worth.

Only Kant's account of the obligatoriness of duties of justice is independent of his account of moral worth. Only in these cases can we explain why certain acts are duties without reference to ends. But we cannot, of course, account for these obligations without reference to the Categorical Imperative and its claim that only a maxim selected on formal grounds avoids heteronomy and so exemplifies a good will. The obligation to act justly is independent of the notion of moral worth, but not of the good will. In Kant's theory the good will is prior to the right and to the morally worthy. But we must beware of seeing in this a retreat from formalism: The goodness of a good will lies simply in its rejection of empirical motives and heteronomy, in its conformity with the moral law as formulated in the Categorical Imperative. Kant's theory can make strong claims to fertility without a retreat from formality.

𝕀 IV *Kant's Theory of Right Action*

Since one part of Kant's theory of right is independent of his theory of moral worth, and the other part dependent, the assessment of that theory divides into two parts. I shall consider first the adequacy of that part of his theory of right action dealing with duties of justice. Kant's theory of justice states that an act is forbidden if its maxim of action cannot consistently be willed as universal law. Acts not forbidden in this sense are permissible; those whose omission is forbidden are obligatory. This account of obligation depends on two sorts of assumption. In the first place, it depends on the justifiability of the Categorical Imperative and of the method of interpreting that principle as applied to maxims of action suggested in chapter 5. The justification is beyond the scope of this book; the interpretation has been fully discussed.

The second sort of assumption on which Kant's theory of right rests is his solution to the problem of relevant descriptions. That solution treats the agent's maxim as being in all circumstances the principle which it is relevant to assess. This solution is not a detachable or dispensable part of Kant's ethical theory. The Categorical Imperative involves the notion of a maxim essentially.[29] The contradictions revealed in unsuccessful attempts to universalize maxims are contradictions between one agent's various simultaneous proposed intentions. There are not in all cases corresponding contradictions between any principles. In the case of most of the examples considered, it was only because an agent's maxim of action and his maxim *qua* universal legislator are both intentions, and so commit the agent to certain further beliefs, that the contradictions were forthcoming. The contradiction in con-

---

[29] One formulation, The Formula of the End in Itself, does not refer to maxims. But the formula cannot be interpreted without such reference.

ception test (like the contradiction in the will test) reveals failures to have coherent intentions.

While the selection of agents' maxims as the principle relevant to assess in determining the obligatoriness (or otherwise) of acts apparently solves the problem of relevant descriptions, it also leads Kant's theory of right to some quite counterintuitive claims. There are many situations in which the universalizability of an agent's maxim does not seem sufficient grounds for assuming an agent's act is either merely permissible or obligatory; and there are situations where the nonuniversalizability of a maxim does not seem sufficient to show an act forbidden. Agents' maxims of action incorporate agents' ignorance, bias, and self-deception. But the rightness and wrongness of acts should not, in the view of most ethical theory or of ordinary opinion, depend on such factors. Some examples may illustrate the variety of counterintuitive judgments of right to which Kant's theory may lead.

A person coming into some money may decide to discharge all his debts, but fail to pay one major creditor because he has forgotten that debt (whether for mundane or for psychologically interesting reasons). No test of his maxim of action would show this omission forbidden. Or a person seeing some lost money in a public place may furtively appropriate it, only to realize later that it had fallen from his own pocket. The permissibility of this act would not be reflected by any test on his maxim.

Another type of situation in which the agent's maxim seems not to be the principle that should be tested in assessment of wrongness and rightness is where that maxim, though not based on ignorance, is in some way "biased." A schoolteacher may intend to treat all the children in his charge fairly, but may classify an act of bullying by a favored pupil as "high spirits," and so give that child a much less severe punishment than he or she gives a less favored child, whose bullying is so described. It is not, we may suppose, false that the favored child was expressing his high spirits—but the description is seriously—"relevantly"—incomplete; it is "biased." Since this bias is incorporated into the agent's maxim, no test of that maxim can show that it was wrong not to treat the two children alike.

Another type of situation in which Kant's theory of right leads either to strange assessments of acts or to none at all is where, though there is no question of ignorance or bias on the agent's part, yet it is hard to know which maxim to assess. Agents may have more than one maxim, causing difficulties for others trying to assess their acts; or agents may have to choose between maxims, which can cause difficulties for them if they are using Kant's theory of right to guide their choice. Cases of the first sort are ones of self-deception; cases of the second sort are ones in which an agent finds "conflicting grounds of obligation."

Consider the case of an elderly and inquisitive woman who often intervenes helpfully but uninvited in neighbors' crises. She realizes that her intentions are mixed, since she tries to disarm others by saying at appropriate times, "Of course, I'm a frightful old busybody but. . . ." Nevertheless, she thinks she is entirely altruistic. She would be genuinely hurt if anyone suggested the contrary. Here we have a case where there is good evidence for attributing either of two maxims to an agent. On one of these her intervention might be judged permissible, and perhaps meritorious; on the other it would be forbidden (it would violate her duty of respect to others). Assuming there is no evidence that either the maxim of intrusion or that of neighborliness is "really" her maxim, it looks as though this situation may raise further problems for Kant's theory of right. In cases of mixed motives or self-deception his solution to the problem of relevant descriptions does not go far enough. It cannot pick out a single principle which it is relevant to assess.

Difficulties of the second sort arise when an agent realizes that of the various maxims of action he might adopt in a given situation two or more are maxims of duty. In any situation an agent can ensure that his maxim is not contrary to duty; and if no maxim of duty appears to apply, he may presumably choose any merely permissible maxim of action. But how is an agent to deal with a situation where he can select between various maxims of duty? Kant describes this situation, but gives no real guidance for those who face it:

There can, it is true, be two *grounds* of obligation . . . both present in one agent and in the rule he lays down for himself. In this case one or the other of these grounds is not sufficient to oblige him . . . and is therefore not a duty.—When two such grounds conflict with each other, practical philosophy says, not that the stronger obligation takes precedence . . . but that the stronger *ground of obligation* prevails.[30]

In such situations we need a procedure for discovering which of two grounds of obligation is stronger, or Kant's ethical theory will not be able to decide which of two possible maxims of action an agent should adopt if he is to carry out his duty.

[30] *M.S.,* p. 223.

There is yet a third type of situation in which Kant's ethical theory seems to lead to unacceptable answers. Though the agent's maxim is neither ignorant, biased nor self-deceiving, and though he has no difficulty in deciding which maxim to adopt, he may slip, bungle, or make some other sort of mistake in acting on his maxim. Success of execution is not irrelevant to the judgments of right; it is irrelevant to the coherence of agents' intentions. A man may fully intend to return a borrowed object to another, and his maxim may be clearly appropriate to the situation. But on the occasion of return he may fall and break the object or mistakenly hand it over to the other man's double, who destroys it. Assuming that such mishaps are entirely unintentional, there is no ground for revising the formulation of the maxim attributed to the agent. Yet assessments of right and wrong based on Kant's ethical theory may lead to surprising results in these cases. In such cases we would usually say that though the agent's intention was to do an act which was right (or wrong), yet he failed to do so. The overall moral assessment of the act would no doubt differ from an assessment of the same result produced by acting on a different maxim. But assessments of right and wrong are not thought to take account of intentions which (for whatever reason) are not implemented. The right road, notoriously, is not the one which is paved with good but unimplemented intentions.

There are also cases in which discrepancies between an agent's maxim of action and his act might not lead us to revise judgments of right and wrong based on Kant's theory of justice. If an agent's ignorance or mistake is the fault of the person whom he wrongs, one might allow a judgment of right or wrong based on assessing the agent's maxim to stand. The situation is more dubious if the ignorance or mistake is the fault not of the person wronged but of a third party. Is a failure to fulfill a contract due to mistaken belief derived from the deliberate deception of a third party wrong?

All the difficulties so far discussed afflict that part of Kant's theory of right which is concerned with duties of justice. We must now consider the case of ethical duties of omission. In determining whether an act violates or fulfills an ethical duty of omission, as in assessing the justice of an act, it is to the agent's maxim of action that we look. But we do not apply the Formula of Universal Law to that maxim. Rather we judge whether the maxim is one of those on which the agent must act if he is not to prevent the realization of some obligatory end. Assuming that Kant has correctly identified obligatory ends, we can see whether acts proposed or undertaken are essential for their realization, will prevent their realization, or are neither essential nor fatal to their realization.

We have already been through some of the ways in which agents' maxims of action can be inappropriate for moral assessment. They may fail to reflect the agent's situation—whether through mistake, bias, or self-deception—or they may not match the act which the agent does when trying to act on them. Maxims on which agents act when they fulfill, or hope to fulfill, ethical duties of omission may suffer from any of these sorts of inappropriateness. But there is also one special, characteristic way in which such maxims may be inappropriate to the agent's situation. Consider the following examples.

Suppose I erroneously believe that taking sulphur baths is essential for health, which is essential if any obligatory ends are to be pursued. Does this show that it is wrong to act on the maxim of omitting sulphur baths? Or suppose that refraining from heavy nicotine addiction is necessary for a reasonable chance of health and longevity, but that an agent will not believe this, whether through lack of understanding or self-deception ("The evidence is only statistical . . ."; "If you're going to get cancer you're going to
. . ."). Can that agent argue that heavy addiction is merely permissible? Or is it wrong? Or suppose that a man persuades himself that his wife is passionately interested in all those sports which he finds absorbing. Can he regard his arrangement of all their spare-time activities to pursue these sports as essential to her happiness and so obligatory? Or is the fact that these activities are not essential to her happiness evidence that his acts are merely permissible, and perhaps even wrong? Or suppose that it is essential for a child's happiness that his friends and relations refrain from reprimanding and criticizing him in public. Do they then do wrong if, not realizing this, they adopt maxims of action leading them to criticize the child in public? Or is such detraction merely permissible?

In such cases the problem is not that the agent's maxim of action is inappropriate for moral assessment. The agent does indeed, as the case may be, take sulphur baths, go on smoking, arrange a season of sporting fixtures, or criticize his child in public. The problem is rather that, because of the erroneous means/ends judgment on which the agent's selection of a maxim of action is based, the agent seems doomed to arrive at an incorrect assessment of the deontic status of his own act. Others who share his erroneous belief may be led to the same mistaken conclusion, but there is no reason to suppose that his mistaken belief will be generally shared.

What we have here is not so much an inadequacy as an oddity in Kant's theory of right: in these cases of acting on an erroneous means/ends judgment it seems as though the agent is at a disadvantage compared to spectators of his act. He may not arrive at a correct assessment of the act's deontic status, yet others may, since in this case they can know the agent's maxim which is the relevant principle for moral assessment. By contrast all the other difficulties afflicting Kant's theory of right affect agents and spectators equally. If the agent's maxim was in any way inappropriate, and so likely to lead the agent to a mistaken assessment of his own act, then it was also not the relevant principle for moral assessment, and so spectators would be left without any method for determining which principle to assess in trying to judge the deontic status of that act.

The conclusions of this section are inauspicious. Kant's theory of justice was shown to be implausible, despite its effectiveness, in all those cases where agents' maxims are inappropriate either to their situation or to their act. His theory of ethical duties of omission was shown to be equally implausible in cases where the agent's maxim is inappropriate to his situation or his act, and plausible only for assessments by others rather than by the agent himself for cases where the maxim, though appropriate to the agent's situation and act, is based on an erroneous means/ends judgment. I shall return to these implausibilities in the next chapter.

V Kant's Theory of Morally Worthy Action

In his theory of moral worth, as in his theory of right, Kant solves the problem of relevant descriptions by taking the agent's maxim as the principle relevant to assess in all cases. Section III of this chapter showed that the maxim of morally worth acts must aim at an objective end. Morally worthy acts must be done to realize a good will, to preserve or promote rational nature, or more restrictedly, to make ourselves more nearly perfect or others happier. They must aim at objective ends because they are such ends, and so be done with the motive of doing one's duty.

This may seem a drastically rigorous, even impossible, theory of morally worthy action, demanding that agents have no ends but that of doing their duty. But this is not so. Agents may in many cases have empirical motives for doing their duty; only if these empirical motives are determining are their actions not morally worthy. There are passages where it seems that Kant does take the more rigorous view:

Suppose [a man] . . . no longer moved by any inclination tears himself out of this deadly insensibility and does the action without any inclination, for the sake of duty alone; then for the first time his action has genuine moral worth.[31]

But the point here is that the man is not *moved* by his inclinations; he may yet have them. Perhaps the reason why one is inclined to read Kant as saying that empirical motives must be absent, rather than that they must not be determining, is that it is easy to think of motives as sorts of pushes or pulls which can never fail to be at least partially determining. But this is to forget Kant's views on human freedom and the role of motives. Motives, in Kant's sense, are something we choose to determine our action. We are not impelled by them. Even when "impulsion" is determining, it is we who have chosen to make it so.

Though Kant's theory of morally worthy action does not demand the absence of empirical motives, it does seem to demand a great deal of men. Kant thinks that morally worthy action is rare and the human heart so impenetrable that we can never be sure whether a given act—our own or another's—is morally worthy. He asks rhetorically:

Who knows himself well enough to say whether the motive for fulfilling his duty proceeds entirely from the thought of the law, or whether there are not many other impulses, of sensuous origin, cooperating with it—motives that look to advantage (or to avoiding disadvantage) and that could in other circumstances just as well serve vice? [32]

Yet the theory does not demand of men that they do the impossible. They do not have to know whether particular acts of their own or others were morally worthy. They simply have to strive to make their acts so. Such striving is within human capacities, even though it may be beyond human capacities to know when the striving is successful.[33]

Clearly we cannot dismiss Kant's theory of morally worthy action on the

[31] *G.*, p. 398.
[32] *M.S.*, p. 446, and cf. *G.*, p. 407. This passage too reflects the deeper difficulties of Kant's account of the relations between the free, rational self and the determined, empirical self.
[33] *M.S.*, p. 446.

ground that it demands the impossible. But we may ask how it compares with what other ethical theories and common opinion say about moral worth. Is Kant's theory of moral worth open to numerous objections of the sort directed to his theory of right action? The difficulty with this question is that opinion on questions of moral worth is both more varied and less often clearly formulated than is opinion on the rightness and wrongness of acts. But the following beliefs about moral worth seem to be fairly widely shared.

Moral worth is ascribed to acts because of their motive or the intentions with which they are done, not (or not solely) because of their deontic status or their results. Moral worth may belong to acts which are obligatory, to acts which are merely permissible, and even perhaps to acts which are forbidden. Similarly, acts with any deontic status may lack moral worth or even be morally unworthy. Disagreement is chiefly over the sort of motive or intention which an act must have in order to be morally worthy. Must it be done from a "feeling of obligation," from "a motive which normally leads to right action," or from one or another of motives such as kindness, respect, courage? Moral worth is perhaps most often attributed to acts because of their "good intentions." But if this judgment is to be part of an ethical theory, we need an analysis of what makes intentions good. Finally, moral worth is something agents can choose to have or to lack. It is not attributable to agents in virtue of circumstances beyond their control.

Kant's theory of moral worth fits the common accounts of moral worth in most respects, and it goes beyond most accounts in giving a precise statement of what it means by "acting with a good intention" or "from a moral motive." His theory ascribes moral worth to actions in virtue of the (usually further) intention with which they are done. This ascription is not dependent on the deontic status of acts or on their results; Kant does allow both for obligatory and for merely permissible acts being morally worthy or lacking moral worth and for forbidden and merely permissible acts being morally unworthy or lacking moral worth.

He does not explicitly allow for acts which are forbidden but morally worthy or for acts which are obligatory yet morally unworthy. But it can be shown that these departures from common accounts of moral worth do not indicate any great inadequacies in his theory of moral worth.

Acts which are forbidden yet morally worthy are typically ones where an agent whose aims are admirable makes some mistake. A clumsy person intending to elicit sympathy for a friend may betray the friend's confidences; a careless person may give away the only means he has to pay a pressing debt. As I said in the criticisms of Kant's theory of right, he pays little attention to the many respects in which an agent's maxim of action may fail to fit the situation, and so, perhaps, fail to be the relevant principle to assess. Kant does not allow for morally worthy but forbidden acts done by mistake because of this. This does not point to a fault in his theory of moral worth, but rather to one in his theory of right. Assessment of the agent's maxim of action in the cases of morally worthy but forbidden acts would show that the act is indeed morally worthy (the agent is aiming at an objective end), but fail to show that it is forbidden, since the agent's maxim of action cannot reveal the mistaken assumption on which he acts—if it could, he would not after all make the mistake.

There are, however, also cases of acts which are morally worthy and forbidden and where no mistake is made. A man may steal to help starving children; he may kill to save innocent lives. He may know what he is doing and that it is forbidden. This case, too, leads back in the end to difficulties in Kant's theory of right. If the man's choice is between violating one or the other of two conflicting obligations—say an obligation to refrain from killing and an obligation to defend others from harm—then we do not know, without a solution to the problem of conflicting grounds of obligation, whether his act is forbidden. If there is no conflict of this sort then the man's adoption of a maxim of action which violates his duty is evidence that he does not (fully) intend the realization of good willing. His maxim of ends is at odds with itself. So his act is not morally worthy. Some other theory of moral worth might account such acts morally worthy, but there do not seem to be any very convincing independent grounds for thinking them so.

The case of acts which are obligatory yet morally unworthy is in many ways parallel. Many acts which seem to fall into this category are ones where the agent does the obligatory act by mistake, in the sense that he acts under some other description. A person may keep a promise to tell another the worst about his illness, but if he has forgotten the promise and does so to put pressure on the other to make his will in the agent's favor and, if possible, hasten his end, the fact that the act fulfills an obligation could not be revealed by Kant's theory of right. The agent's maxim of action is to tell the other the worst about his prospects of recovery; he does not act under the description of keeping his promise. Another example of this kind would be that of a contractor who delivers cement inferior to that specified in an order with the hope of increasing his profit. If the order has been altered and specifies inferior cement, the agent's intention is still not to fulfill the contract, but he in fact does so. Yet assessing his maxim of action cannot show that he did an obligatory act. In these cases of mistaken fulfillments of obligations, Kant's theory of right fails to show the act obligatory, though it can show the agent's purpose (in each case to harm another for some presumed gain) incompatible with the pursuit of objective ends, and so morally unworthy.

Where an agent intentionally does an obligatory act in pursuit of a morally unworthy end, Kant's theory of right can deal with the situation. A man might intentionally discharge a debt to another (which is obligatory), but do so to embarrass or rebuff the other. There is no reason why applying the Categorical Imperative to his maxims of action and of ends should not show these acts obligatory and morally unworthy. Kant's ethical theory can allow for such acts, though he gives no examples.

Kant can therefore allow for some but not all cases where virtuous intentions lead to forbidden deeds and some but not all cases where there is wicked meaning in a lawful deed. The cases for which he cannot allow are those in which the act description of the agent's maxim is not that under which the act is forbidden or lawful. In each case the difficulty can be attributed to one of the shortcomings of his theory of right discussed in the previous section of this chapter, and not to anything amiss with his theory of moral worth. Kant's ethical theory can quite easily account for all cases of this sort where the agent's maxim of action is not in some way inappropriate to the situation.

Kant's theory of moral worth, therefore, meets the most substantial conditions usually required of theories of moral worth. Even so, some might object that there are more motives than reverence for the law, more ends than the system of objective ends which can make an act morally worthy. Why should not certain sorts of ends desired make acts morally worthy? Acts done from empirical motives such as love or respect seem plausible candidates for the status of morally worthy acts. But Kant argues explicitly against this line of thought. Moral worth cannot be something which one man may effortlessly have, because of his amiable disposition, while another lacks it for reasons beyond his control.

Love out of inclination cannot be commanded; but kindness done from duty—although no inclination impels us, and even although natural and unconquerable disinclination stands in our way—is *practical*, and not *pathological*, love, residing in

the will and not in the propensions of feeling, in principles of action and not of melt-
ing compassion; and it is this practical love alone which can be an object of command.[34]

Moral worth must be something that a man may decide to pursue, and he
cannot choose his empirical motives, only his maxims; hence moral worth
must be determined by his maxims. There is certainly no basis for thinking
that Kant's theory of morally worthy acts requires that those acts be ones
which we have no inclination to do; but they cannot derive their moral
worth from the fact that we are inclined to do them. Benevolent inclinations
are amiable and beautiful, but they do not merit moral praise. All ethical assessments, including assessments of moral worth, assess aspects of acts for
which agents can be held responsible.

Given how vague theories of moral worth tend to be, one can still ask
whether there are cases where defects similar to those found in Kant's theory
of right in the previous section of this chapter might arise. Are there situations where it seems that an agent's maxim of ends is not the principle which
it is relevant and appropriate to assess in judging the moral worth of his act?
Can maxims of ends be ignorant, biased, or self-deceiving? Can agents slip,
bungle, or make other sorts of mistakes in acting on their maxims of ends?

The answers to these questions require a lot of care in distinguishing
complete from incomplete maxims of ends. Agents act only on the former.
Any incomplete maxim of ends must be supplemented by a maxim of action
if the agent is to act on his maxim. But in assessing the moral worth or lack
thereof of acts according to Kant's ethical theory, it is incomplete maxims of
ends which must be considered. It is not relevant to the moral worth of an
agent's act that he chooses a maxim of action which will not or cannot lead
to the end at which he aims, or which is biased or self-deceiving. Provided
the agent's maxim of ends is known, everything needed to assess the moral
worth of his act is available.

This last proviso glosses over many difficulties. Our evidence for attributing maxims of ends to agents is in large part based on consideration of what
their acts and imputed maxims of action tend to. Agents do not always avow
their maxims of ends, and if they do they may not have the last word on the
matter. Actions speak louder than words here. It is possible to make sense of
the notion of a mistaken, biased, or self-deceiving maxim of ends in the

---

[34] *G.*, p. 399.

sense of a mistaken, biased, or self-deceiving complete maxim of ends. A person might aim to help others and do so by sedulous discussion of their shortcomings. It is imaginable that he mistakenly thinks this the most effective means to his ends, that he misdescribes his course of action as, say, "going over the problem," or that his true purpose is to reassure himself by dwelling on the inadequacies of others. Only the details of particular case histories could decide between these possibilities.

Only the last of these possibilities—where the agent's avowed purpose and his true purpose differ—has any bearing on the moral worth of the agent's act. Only if the evidence of action, and other circumstantial evidence, is sufficient to require revision of an imputed incomplete maxim of ends does it bear on the question of moral worth. The occasional choice of inappropriate means, whether due to ignorance or bias in describing the means, has in itself no effect on the moral worth of an act—though it may be very important in determining whether an agent has fulfilled his ethical duties of omission.

When the end imputed must be altered in the light of action undertaken there is room not merely for the case of conflicting evidence (avowal vs. action) but for genuine self-deception about ends. Where the conflict is simply that different parts of the available evidence point in different directions, the conflict may be resolved by seeking further evidence to establish that one or other possible incomplete maxims of ends is the one attributable to the agent on this occasion and which therefore should be assessed in coming to judgments of moral worth. In particular contexts it may, of course, be impossible to acquire decisive evidence, and in such cases any assessment of moral worth must be tentative. But there are also cases where the unavailability of such evidence shows that the agent aims at two ends which are incompatible, not just in the sense that in some situations both cannot be pursued (that sort of incompatibility might arise for almost any pair of ends), but in the sense that there are no situations in which both could be realized. Even when ends are incompatible in this strong sense, agents may aim at both. A person might aim both to treat his wife as an equal and to protect her from all knowledge about their true economic circumstances. These policies are not compatible. Someone who is shielded is not treated as an equal. In such cases the agent has—whether one end is pursued and one avowed, or whether both are partially pursued and both avowed—an incoherent maxim of ends. A person in this situation is not merely presenting conflicting evidence about his ends; he is deceiving himself.

What can Kant's theory of moral worth say about such cases? What would an application of the contradiction in the will test to a self-deceiving maxim of ends show? In the above example it would show the man's aims morally unworthy, for he intends and can intend no set of means sufficient to realize his two ends. His intentions are incoherent, and thus morally unworthy. The same result would be achieved by applying the contradiction in the will test to any other case of self-deceiving maxims of ends. Such maxims are all ones in which the agent intends two (or more) ends (including as a special case the realization of a certain end and its nonrealization) that could not in any circumstances be jointly realized. Hence, he cannot intend any set of means sufficient for their joint realization (unless he makes some further sort of mistake), and so cannot have coherent intentions. Self-deception in the pursuit of ends is a violation of duty; self-knowledge a duty. Kant's theory of moral worth can deal with these cases where an agent's maxim of ends is *prima facie* inappropriate for assessing the moral worth of his act.

The last group of examples which caused difficulties for Kant's theory of right were those in which, though the agent's maxim of action was the appropriate principle for assessments of right, yet his action on the maxim was in some way defective or unsuccessful. There is no analogous class of difficult cases facing Kant's theory of moral worth. The moral worth of acts is independent of agents' success either in acting on their maxims of action or in realizing their aims. Provided those aims are morally worthy (or unworthy or lacking in moral worth) and are genuinely the aims of the agents, their acts are morally worthy (or unworthy or lacking in moral worth). Striving for moral worthy ends, not achieving them, is the criterion of morally worthy action.

Kant's theory of moral worth seems to be exempt from the sorts of internal defect that flaw his theory of right action. If his theory of moral worth is inadequate, this must be because his analysis of moral worth in terms of aiming only at ends at which one can coherently intend others to aim is defective. Kant's solution to the problem of relevant descriptions seems to cause no difficulties for his theory of moral worth. Any difficulties which can be found in that theory—and I have argued that it is free from the more obvious defects that a theory of moral worth must avoid—could be attributable only to some flaw in the requirements of the Categorical Imperative and their justification.

CHAPTER SEVEN

RIGHT DECISIONS
AND ASSESSMENTS OF RIGHT

Chapter 6 showed some of the ways in which Kant's solution to the problem of relevant descriptions produces difficulties for his theory of right. Where an agent does not match his maxim to the situation or his act to his maxim, where he acts on an erroneous means/ends judgment, and where he faces conflicting grounds of obligation, it seems that Kant's theory of right might give either unacceptable guidance or none at all. By contrast his theory of moral worth did not get into such difficulties.

These conclusions are surprising and, at first glance, disappointing. Other universalizability tests have been proposed primarily as necessary or necessary and sufficient conditions on principles of right. Though Hare speaks of his test as proposing a necessary condition on *all* moral judgments, he has in mind primarily "ought judgments"; Singer explicitly restricts his discussion to principles of right and wrong. A theory of right has come to seem to many writers on ethics the basic and indispensable kernel of an ethical theory, to which theories of moral worth or of supererogation or of virtue are always ancillary. If Kant lacks a theory of right he has at most fragments of an ethical theory to offer.

Before accepting this gloomy conclusion, it is worth remembering that only some applications of Kant's theory of right ran into difficulties. As the sample derivations of chapter 5 showed, the contradiction in conception test leads to intuitively acceptable results if it is applied only to "appropriate" principles. Kant's solution to the problem of relevant descriptions seems adequate except for this minority of cases. The problems arise when agents have difficulty in choosing a maxim of action and when the maxims chosen are inappropriate to the situation or to the act done. A partial solution to these problems can be given by a reinterpretation and supplementation of Kant's theory.

I Contexts of Action and Contexts of Assessment

Consider first the case of an agent who has no difficulty in choosing and formulating a maxim, but doubts whether his maxim is the appropriate principle for him to test if he is to discover the deontic status of his proposed act. He fears that his maxim may be in some way based upon ignorance, misconception, or bias, or that he may be deceiving himself in formulating it. Even if none of these is true, he may fear that the act he will do may not live up to his maxim. He may muff the execution and fail to do what he intends. What can an agent in this sort of situation do?

There is no general answer to this question. He should exercise caution and judgment, reviewing his knowledge of the facts and the credentials of his informants. In acting he should proceed attentively and with forethought—and so on. This is not to say that agents in this situation should move slowly or hesitantly. Sometimes the right act must be done quickly or even spontaneously; but even these cases will require that the agent exercise judgment, in the most general sense of that term. Without this sort of approach, an application of the contradiction in conception test or of the test for ethical duties of omission may simply mislead. The qualities of character necessary to proceed in this way are repeatedly emphasized by Kant. The moral agent must above all be free from self-deception, conscientious and self-knowing: "Moral self-knowledge, which requires one to penetrate into the unfathomable depths and abyss of one's heart is the beginning of all human wisdom." [1]

This emphasis on judgment and self-knowledge may, one supposes, minimize the number of occasions on which an agent's maxim is inappropriate. But it does not seem to strike at the heart of the problem. Due care and judgment cannot ensure that maxims will always be appropriate to situations, or that acts done on them will not depart or fall short of the maxims in some way. The question remains whether the agent's maxim of action is always the principle which should be assessed to discover an act's deontic status.

[1] M.S., p. 440.

Yet this way of stating the question is also misleading. We need to distinguish the question whether it is always appropriate for an agent to test his own maxim and the question whether it is always appropriate for spectators to assess the agent's maxim. What is appropriate in the context of assessment may not always be appropriate in a context of action or decision.

In the previous chapter the criticisms of Kant's theory of right which depended on pointing out the possibility of the agent's maxim failing to fit either his situation or his act were all made from the bird's-eye viewpoint of a context of assessment. It was assumed that it could be discovered when an agent's maxim was inappropriate to his situation or to his act, or when the agent was acting on the basis of a mistaken means/ends judgment. But when we act we are not in that position. Once all reasonable care has been taken to avoid ignorance, bias, or self-deception, an agent can do nothing more to determine that his maxim does not match his situation. Once an agent has acted on his maxim attentively, he can do no more to ensure that his act lives up to his maxim. We cannot choose to succeed, but only to strive. Once he has taken due care to get his means/ends judgments right, he can do nothing further to ensure that they are right. Agents are not simultaneously their own spectators. In contexts of action they cannot go behind their own maxims and beliefs. We can make right decisions, but not guarantee right acts.

Nor, of course, can every spectator go behind an agent's maxims and beliefs. Usually they will be far less informed about agents' situations, beliefs, and acts than are agents themselves, for all their possible bias and mistakes. But when an agent is biased, mistaken, or self-deceiving, in spite of having taken all reasonable care to be none of these, it is not even possible that he should, at that time, realize the inappropriateness of his maxim to his situation, or the error of a means/ends judgment on which he bases the performance of some ethical duty of omission, or that he should foresee that his act will not be what he intends. If he did uncover his bias, mistake, or self-deception, he would either revise his maxim or have to find new grounds for retaining it. By contrast, a spectator may be able to see the inappropriateness of an agent's maxim to his situation, to discover the erroneous means/ends judgment leading an agent to, say, make a duty of taking sulphur baths, or to foresee an impending divergence between maxim and act.

On the other hand, in contexts of having acted agents are their own spectators. Like others they may be able to see a discrepancy between maxim and situation, an error in their previous means/ends judgments, or a discrepancy between maxim and act. They are no longer in a context of action, but in one of assessment.

So there is a distinction between contexts of action and contexts of assessment. In the former, if all care and attention have already been exercised, nothing more can be done to learn whether the maxim of action tested to discover an act's deontic status was one which incorporated the relevant composite act description and was not based on an erroneous means/ends judgment. In the latter context further steps can often be taken to see whether there is not some sort of hiatus between maxim and situation, between means/ends judgments and the probable causal sequences, or between maxim and act. The question we can now raise is whether an ethical theory—in particular, a theory of right—should be designed to function in a context of action or of assessment, or in both.

Some recent ethical theories have assumed that it is the context of assessment for which theories of right are primarily designed. This is most explicit in various moral point of view or "ideal spectator" theories, which contend that agents should test their proposed action by disregarding the fact that they are agents and taking a special sort of spectator's view of the situation. Insofar as this means no more than that agents should be attentive and judicious in certain specified ways in deciding what to do, this is compatible with the fact that the agent is in a context of action. But if it is taken to mean that agents ought to discover any inappropriateness in their maxim and forestall any shortcoming in their act, this assumes they should make their decisions in a context of assessment. This is to demand more than is possible. Contexts of action cannot, I have just argued, be reduced to contexts of assessment. Agents cannot be required to do more than exercise care and attention.

Other recent ethical theories have assimilated the two contexts and regard the agent and spectator as being basically in the same position. A single theory should be able to guide our moral choices and enable us to assess the rightness and wrongness of others' deeds. Both Hare and Singer make these assumptions. Yet it is quite possible that a theory which can be used effectively in one context will not work in the other.

The criticisms in the last section all showed that Kant's theory of right could not function acceptably in all contexts of assessment, but these criticisms do not hold for contexts of action. Where the inappropriateness of an agent's maxim to his situation is discoverable, testing his maxim may well not lead to a correct, or even to a plausible, assessment of the deontic status of the act. But in contexts of decision Kant's theory does provide adequate guidance. Agents cannot do better than to act on carefully vetted maxims. If their act conforms to a maxim which can be shown obligatory or permissible, whether by the test for duties of justice or by that for ethical duties of omission, then they can do no more to ensure that their act is obligatory or permissible. Others may discover the inappropriateness of the maxim; the agent cannot and so cannot be required to make this discovery. Kant's theory of right is not in fact open to the sorts of counterexample which arise from agents' ignorance, bias, or self-deception. But it is a theory which tells us how to decide rightly rather than whether acts are right.

But should not a complete theory of right be able to guide our action and our assessments? Is not a reinterpretation of Kant's theory of right as a theory for deciding on acts rightly rather than a method for picking out the right act a great retreat from the aim of rational ethics, and so quite un-Kantian in spirit? Do we not need a theory which enables us to tell, not merely whether agents have decided rightly, but also whether they have made the right decision? Must not an adequate solution to the problem of relevant descriptions be a theory of moral relevance which works in all contexts?

The retreat is not as great as suggested. Consider the contrast between Kant's theory of right and an existentialist position. A Kantian moral agent, like the existentialist, will not readily pass judgment on others, for he can never be sure whether the other's maxim of action is the principle which he should assess. In the first place it may be hard to determine what that maxim is, but, more importantly, it may not be the maxim he as spectator thinks relevant to assess in judging that act done in that situation. Yet he has no method by which to determine what other principle of action should be assessed. In this sense a Kantian moral agent will not legislate for others.

But when a Kantian agent faces a moral problem himself he will regard his decision as backed by an argument which would have precisely the same force for any other agent in his situation. The Kantian agent will have taken all due care to make sure that his maxim is appropriate to his situation and that no erroneous means/ends beliefs affect his choice of maxim. And he fully intends to act on his maxim. Any other agent in his position would find the same argument able to guide him in determining whether his act was required either by justice or as an ethical duty of omission. Decision is not king in Kant's ethical theory. There is far more to his position than an emphasis on the autonomy of moral agents.

A Kantian moral agent is committed to judging an act done on the same maxim by another agent in his position and sharing his beliefs as having the same deontic status as his own act. In this sense he does legislate for others. The point at which he hesitates is in regarding another's act as being the same as his own in all respects. He legislates for those hypothetical agents who do what he does. But since he knows that there may be some fault or flaw in his perception of acts and situations, he will not apply his legislation to other agents however similar their acts may appear to him. He can offer others moral advice or point out what seem to him relevant facts. But if they persist in viewing their act differently and assessing a maxim which differs from the one he assesses, he has no method (normal methods of rational discourse having, we presume, failed to persuade either party to relinquish his view) of showing that the two acts are the same, and must both have the deontic status he assigns to his own act.

Another interesting comparison may be made between Kant's theory of right and certain models of rational choice.[2] A model of rational choice may be characterized very generally as a procedure by which an agent facing a number of possible courses of action to each of whose possible outcomes he assigns some value, can choose between these courses of action. More formally, if $A_1, A_2, \ldots, A_n$ are possible courses of action, and the values assigned to the possible outcomes of each A_i are represented by $u_{i1}, u_{i2}, \ldots, u_{im}$, we have an $n \times m$ array:

$$
\begin{array}{ll}
A_1 & u_{11}, u_{12}, \ldots, u_{1m} \\
A_2 & u_{21}, u_{22}, \ldots, u_{2m} \\
\ \ \vdots & \qquad \vdots \\
A_n & u_{n1}, u_{n2}, \ldots, u_{nm}
\end{array}
$$

The agent choosing between $A_1, \ldots, A_n$ can adopt any of a number of algorithms of rational choice, depending on the further knowledge available to him. If, for instance, he knows the probability distribution, $p_1, \ldots, p_m$

[2] For a survey of such models cf. R. D. Luce and H. Raiffa, *Games and Decisions,* especially chs. 2 and 13, pp. 12–38, 275–326.

for each u_{i1}, . . . , u_{im}, given that he chooses A_i, he might act on the algorithm of maximizing his expected utility. He could choose that A_i which maximizes $u_{i1}P_1 + u_{i2}P_2 + \ldots + u_{im}P_m$. If, on the other hand, he knew only which outcomes were possible for any given choice, A_i, but could assign no numerical probabilities, though he could assign utility numbers to these outcomes, he might act on the minimax principle and select that A_i for which the least-valued possible outsome was greatest.

Such models are all highly idealized in the assumptions they make about agents' knowledge of outcomes and their probabilities, about agents' capacity to assign numbers to their valuation of each outcome, and about agents' computational capacity. This defect has led Simon [3] to suggest that one might devise a very different sort of model of rational choice for actual human agents. Agents might, for instance, operate on the algorithm of selecting the first A_i they considered that had at least one u_{ij} which the agent judged satisfactory. (Alternatively the agent might choose the first A_i such that at least one of u_{i1}, . . . , u_{im} is satisfactory and has a probability of occurrence, given A_i, which is greater than some preassigned critical value.) Such an algorithm describes a procedure by which agents may "satisfice," though the choice they make by following the procedure may well not be optimal as judged in a context of greater information and computational skill.

An analogy can now be drawn between a theory of deciding rightly such as Kant's theory of right, under the interpretation I have given, and a model, such as satisficing, which suggests a computational procedure that, though not optimal in the abstract, may be the best attainable by agents in "nonoptimal" conditions. An agent following the algorithm of satisficing may not make that choice which would be defined as the rational choice from a bird's-eye viewpoint of complete information about utilities and probabilities. But we may still judge that he has chosen rationally if the complete information is unavailable or very costly (in terms of energy, time, or money). Similarly we can regard Kant's theory of right as providing a theory by which an agent who knows that his view of the situation may be imperfect can choose rightly.

The difference between the two procedures is that we can contrast the choice of the satisficer with the rational choice that might have been made in a situation of idealized knowledge. But we cannot contrast the choice of an agent who decides rightly with the right decision that some complete Kan-

[3] M. Simon, *Models of Man,* especially introduction and ch. 14.

tian theory of right would provide. Kant's theory of right does not provide any method for determining the relevant composite act description under which to assess an act when we take the bird's-eye view of a context of assessment. I shall consider some suggestions which might repair this omission in his theory of right in the last section of this chapter.

II Conflicting Grounds of Obligation

One difficulty for Kant's theory of right raised in the previous chapter survives the reinterpretation just given. In contexts of action, agents may face conflicting grounds of obligation between which they must choose. This problem will arise only in certain quite precisely specifiable sorts of situation.

A theory of right for use in contexts of action does not have to select a maxim for agents to adopt in any given situation. Such a demand is beyond the scope of a theory of right. We cannot hope to have a method for generating all those maxims which an agent might adopt in a given situation, to each of which the test of rightness can then be applied. A preliminary selection of the choice set of maxims must be determined by such factors as the interest, knowledge, desires, and means/ends judgments of agents. In this Kant's theory of right is no more inadequate than any other—utilitarian theories cannot seriously demand that we consider the expected utility of all possible courses of action. Hare does not seriously envisage moral agents running over all the moral judgments they might make in a given situation, rather he explicitly mentions the importance of various constraints of context in setting the scene for moral choice. Judgment and thought are no doubt needed in drawing up a preliminary choice set of maxims, if maxims of possible moral significance are not to be omitted from the list. But there is no method beyond the common or garden ones for ensuring that the choice set will not exclude some maxims of this sort.

Once given a rough-and-ready preliminary listing of possible maxims of action, a theory of right should be able to take over and discriminate among these. Kant's theory of right can perform most of those discriminations necessary to guide action. It can classify maxims of action as proposing acts which may not be done, acts which may be done, and acts which it is obligatory to do. In the latter case a difficulty can arise. For logical or empirical reasons, it may be impossible to adopt all those maxims of action which are obligatory. For this reason Kant, when speaking strictly, considers maxims as laying down only grounds of obligation, never obligations:

> . . . a conflict of duties and obligations is inconceivable . . . But there can, it is true, be two *grounds* of obligation . . . both present in one agent and in the rule he lays down for himself. In this case one or other of the grounds is not sufficient to oblige him . . . and is therefore not a duty.[4]

The problem may be stated in more modern terms, without much distortion, as that of determining which of two *prima facie* duties is an actual duty.[5] In Kantian terminology the problem is to discover the stronger of two grounds of obligation.

In many cases of apparently conflicting grounds of obligation, the conflict is easily resolvable. A man may have a debt to pay in one place and an appointment to honor in another. He cannot simultaneously fulfill the two obligations. But he can do so successively. This is a sort of conflict of grounds of obligation which need cause no worry.

A difficulty arises where the adoption of one *prima facie* obligatory maxim is incompatible with the adoption of another. We may as well use an example of Kant's in considering the case. In *Über Ein Vermeintes Recht aus Menschenliebe zu Lügen* he discusses the case of lying to save the life of the intended victim of a would-be murderer. The situation is this: The would-be murderer asks the householder where his intended victim is and reveals his intentions. The householder knows the victim's whereabouts and can choose between lying to mislead the murderer or directing him to his victim.

In his essay on the case Kant argues for the overriding duty of truth telling. Commentators have agreed that Kant's solution is repugnant and uncharacteristic, but have not satisfactorily explained what his solution should have been. Paton,[6] for instance, points out that Kant's ethical theory

---

[4] *M.S.*, p. 223.

[5] "I suggest 'prima facie duty' . . . as a brief way of referring to the characteristic . . . which an act has, . . . in virtue of being of a certain kind, of being an act which would be a duty proper if it were not at the same time of another kind which is morally significant." D. Ross, *The Right and the Good,* p. 19. If we take "being of another morally significant kind" as being an act which will violate the other ground of obligation, the two distinctions are equivalent.

[6] H. J. Paton, "An Alleged Right to Lie: A Problem in Kantian Ethics," *Kant-Studien,* Vol. 45, 1953–54.

does not commit him to general principles in the sense of abstract rather than specific principles, but to universal principles which may incorporate any amount of detail. "To tell the truth" does not have to take precedence over the more specific "To tell the truth only if it will not lead to someone being killed." Though it is quite true that Kant's position does not so commit him, this is in itself no solution to the problem of conflicting grounds of obligation. That problem may also be posed as one of choosing between maxims of equal specificity. Should an agent choose to tell the truth if it will not lead to someone being killed or to prevent someone's being killed if it can be done without lying?

When an agent is faced with a conflict situation he is able to act on only one of any pair (or larger number) of conflicting grounds of obligation. In this situation his maxim of action with respect to the two grounds of obligation, say x and y, will have to be either

A. To do x even if it means omitting y

or

B. To do y even if it means omitting x,

unless, of course, he chooses to flout both grounds of obligation. But how is an agent to choose between a pair of maxims whose forms are A and B? Is x or y the stronger ground of obligation?

No simple attempt to adapt the contradiction in conception test to this situation can work. That test was designed to determine not whether something was a "stronger" or "weaker" ground of obligation, but simply whether it was an obligation.

Nevertheless, a very similar test can often be of some use to agents who face conflicting grounds of obligation. Between any two maxims of forms A and B, there will often be greater difficulty in universalizing one according to the contradiction in conception test than there is in universalizing the other. Some examples will illustrate the way in which universalizing, though not impossible, can be difficult.

An agent faced with the dilemma of Kant's householder must choose between:

1. To tell the truth even if it means allowing (omitting to prevent) a death,

and

2. To prevent a death even if it means telling a lie.

The UTC's of these maxims are

3. Everyone will tell the truth even when it means allowing deaths.

4. Everyone will prevent deaths even when it means telling lies.

It is possible without contradiction to intend both 1 and that 3 hold as a law of nature, and to intend both 2 and that 4 hold as a law of nature. But there is a great difference between the two cases. In the case of 2 and 4, simultaneous intending produces no difficulties. No serious breakdown of trust or cooperation with others will arise if we know that others will lie when it is required to save a life. But in the case of simultaneously intending 1 and 3, we would intend such a breakdown of trust and cooperation. If we know that others will not tell a lie even to save a life, then we can hardly trust them in any situation of potential danger. Intending 1 and 3 commits an agent to intending a situation which tends toward a Hobbesian state of nature, and so tends to impede or prevent all plans of action, including that envisaged in 1. Our cooperation with others would have to be carefully limited in such a situation. This difference in the results of universalizing 1 and 2 may be taken as the basis for calling 2 the stronger ground of obligation.

This extension of the contradiction in conception test does not introduce utilitarian considerations. The reason for classifying as a duty action on whichever of a pair of maxims that balances conflicting grounds of obligation and has a UTC tending to produce a less extreme state of nature is, not that more extreme states of nature are more undesirable, but that no rational agent will intend both an avoidable state of nature and a plan of action. A Hobbesian state of nature does not preclude all planned action, but it makes it all uncertain. So the priority of conflicting grounds of obligation can be determined by seeing which of the two maxims balancing them tends more toward a state of nature when universalized.

This criterion is not to be found in Kant's works, though it is obviously derivative from them. Nor is it razor sharp. But then we should not perhaps expect it to be so. It has the merits of filling a gap in Kant's theory of right decisions and of yielding results which generally confirm our intuitions. That is to say, it generally accounts stronger those grounds of obligation which we think of as being so, weaker those grounds of obligation which we think of as relatively trivial, while failing to indicate any priority between grounds of obligation which we probably regard as pressing claims of similar urgency.

Further examples will bear this out. Consider the pair of maxims:

5. I will be punctual even if it means allowing deaths.

6. I will prevent deaths even if it makes me late.

A system of nature characterized by the UTC of 5 would be one in which trust and cooperation between men would be deeply marred by the knowledge that others would always allow a trivial requirement of punctuality to override matters of life and death. Such a system of nature would tend toward the Hobbesian state of nature, and so to making it impossible to act on 5.

On the other hand, a system of nature characterized by the UTC of 6 would not have such difficulties. Consider also the pair of maxims:

7. I will pay my debts even if it means breaking a contract.

8. I will keep all contracts even if it means leaving some debt unpaid.

Neither a situation characterized by the UTC of 7 nor by the UTC of 8 seems decisively closer to collapse into a Hobbesian state of nature than the other. This is what we might expect of an attempt to use this method to adjudicate between conflicting grounds of obligation which are *prima facie* of similar importance. If, on the other hand, the maxims were to indicate that the debt is trivial and the contract vital, or *vice versa,* then some difference between the systems of nature characterized by the UTC's of the two maxims should be discernible.

All these patterns of argument have one form: they show that the situation characterized by the UTC of one or the other of two maxims of forms A and B will approximate more toward a Hobbesian state of nature. The situations characterized by the UTC's of the maxims described as more difficult to universalize will not usually be Hobbesian states of nature. They will characterize situations in which agents still can often, but not reliably, act on maxims and fulfill their intentions. Universalizing a maxim which makes the weaker of two grounds of obligation override the stronger will not lead to a contradiction. But it will lead to a less coherent set of intentions, which can serve agents who find themselves faced with conflicting grounds of obligation as a guide.

✻ III Assessments of Right

I have so far argued that Kant has, beside his theory of moral worth, a theory of right which makes reasonably precise and plausible discriminations, provided it is used only in contexts of action. I want now to investigate whether it can be adapted to assessing others' acts. Such an adaptation would be a departure from Kant's theory, which chapter 6 showed was unsuitable for contexts of assessment where there may be reasons for denying that the agent's maxim is relevant for moral assessment.

Various other solutions to the problem of relevant descriptions have been proposed, not always as adjuncts of particular ethical theories. Some of these may yield a solution to the problem of relevant descriptions which is appropriate for all contexts. I shall consider some of these proposals briefly.

One proposal, which I have not seen canvassed but which might be considered first, is this: There is no need to get at the morally relevant description of an act to decide whether to do it or how to assess it. Morally relevant act descriptions are just those composite act descriptions which occur in moral principles. So in assessing a particular act all one need do is to run through the various composite descriptions of the act and see which, if any, of these occur in moral principles. *Ex post facto* one may call these descriptions morally relevant descriptions of the act. But we do not have to be able to single out the morally relevant description or descriptions of an act before we assess it morally.

But to suppose that we can find the morally relevant descriptions of acts in this way, i.e., in the course of assessing them morally, is to assume that we can generate all the composite descriptions of an act and then see which, if any, of these fall under a (presumably finite) list of moral principles. But how could one generate and then run through the set of all composite descriptions of a given act? Composite act descriptions may, and usually do, incorporate reference to the circumstances and consequences of acting. Any act has an indefinitely large set of circumstances, and conceivably an indefinitely large set of consequences. Hence we can, at most, test some subset of the composite descriptions of an act to see whether any of them falls under a moral principle.

How is this subset of composite act descriptions of a given act to be generated? Intuitively, we want to exclude from the composite act descriptions in the subset reference to the act's remoter circumstances and consequences. But how is "remote" to be interpreted here? Clearly we do not want to say that circumstances remote in time or space cannot figure in the composite act descriptions in this subset. Whether the person against whom I bear false witness is here or in Australia, whether radioactive contamination will damage the health of this generation or of their great-grandchildren, are not the sorts of distinction on which membership of the set of morally relevant composite act descriptions of a given act should be based. In the case of remote consequences, "remote" might also be interpreted to mean "improbable." But we also do not want automatically to debar moral assessment of acts under all descriptions which incorporate a reference to remotely possible, or improbable, consequences. Act descriptions such as "administering a drug which has a .01 likelihood of causing blindness" are not the sort we want to fail to assess morally. In fact it does not seem likely that the task of determining the relevant description of an act for purposes of moral assessment can be avoided in the way suggested. Any method for cutting down the number of descriptions under which the act would have to be assessed to some manageable finite number either fails to do the right job or simply involves an implicit theory of moral relevance.

An explicit theory of morally relevant act descriptions was provided by Lyons in *Forms and Limits of Utilitarianism.* Though he did not claim to have set out a mechanical method for determining the morally relevant descriptions of an act, the procedure he suggests is feasible. He calls that act description morally relevant which consists of the conjunction of all those descriptions mentioning a feature of the act in virtue of which it tends to have desirable or undesirable consequences. But this sort of solution to the problem of relevant descriptions is justifiable only within some sort of utilitarian context. Only if we suppose that the moral status of acts depends on that of their consequences will act descriptions which mention those consequences (or those of them with nonzero utility) be all and only the morally relevant act descriptions. Lyons' solution to the problem of relevant descriptions cannot reasonably be combined with Kant's universality test, since that test is intended to determine the moral status of acts without any reference to their results.

A third approach to the problem of relevant descriptions is suggested by Anscombe in her discussion of intentions.[7] She first points out that a certain subset of the descriptions of an act can be characterized as intentional act descriptions. An intentional act description may be cited in answer to the question "What are you doing?" and can also be further questioned by "Why are you doing that?" (Nonintentional act descriptions, on the other hand, cannot be given in answer to "What are you doing?" and if queried with "Why are you doing that?" can only be met with responses such as "I did not realize I was.")[8]

The various intentional act descriptions of one act can be arranged in a series, or in a number of series, say a, b, c, d, such that each description applies to the act in virtue of the holding of a more complex set of circumstances than the application of its predecessor required. A single act may be characterizable as moving the arm, pumping water, replenishing a water supply, and poisoning the inhabitants of a house. Moving the arm is, given certain other circumstances, pumping; pumping is, given certain circumstances, replenishing the water supply, which again, given certain further circumstances, is poisoning the inhabitants. Anscombe characterizes the relation of each description to its successor as one of means to ends, it being understood that they describe not successive intentional acts but rather an increasing proportion of the components of one intentional act. The last term of a series of intentional act descriptions such as the example given states, she thinks, the intention with which the agent acts. This marks it out from its predecessors. The description in position d can be mentioned in answer to any question "Why?" about those descriptions in position a, b, or c. In Anscombe's example the sequence ends with the intentional act description which appears relevant for any sort of moral assessment.[9]

How generally can one take an intentional act description that states the intention with which the agent acts as the relevant description for moral assessments, and in particular for assessments of right? The answer is depressing. In the first place, we sometimes wish to assess the rightness of acts under nonintentional descriptions. In cases where agents are ignorant, biased, or self-deceiving, or when they muff the execution of the act they

[7] G. E. M. Anscombe, *Intention*.   [8] *Ibid.*, pp. 37–40.
[9] *Ibid.*, pp. 45–47.

propose, the act description which seems most relevant for assessments of right may be nonintentional. Here Anscombe's solution to the problem of relevant descriptions is no advance on Kant's.

Second, her criterion is not easy to apply. If I spend a proportion of my money on horse races, my act can be characterized by intentional act descriptions such as: checking out a racing sheet; placing a bet; gambling y amount of money on the chance of winning z amount. But the last of these intentional act descriptions cannot (if I am the usual sort of gambler) be described as the intention with which I act. I bet to win, not to gamble. The intention with which I act is that of (perhaps) winning z amount of money. But this is not a description, let alone an intentional description, of my act. I cannot, alas, answer the question "What are you doing?" by "Winning z amount of money." Anscombe herself points out that only as a joke would we cite a doubtful or remote objective as an intentional description of an act.[10] I may aim to win money on the horses, but that is not what I am doing when I place my bet. So we have here a case where the intention with which the agent acts is not included among the intentional descriptions of his act. Here the proposed criterion cannot select one act description as relevant for moral assessment.

Third, Anscombe's position sometimes seems to mislead. The description most relevant for moral assessment can be one of the "means" terms rather than the "end" term in a series of intentional act descriptions each of which applies in virtue of the holding of more specific circumstances than the application of its predecessor required. Suppose an employer fires an employee who has a dependent family, with the intention of providing summer employment for the son of a business associate. In this case, not only the act description that states the intention with which the agent acts, but also the other intentional act description would seem to be relevant for any sort of moral assessment. More generally we do not want to restrict moral assessment to a single aspect of any given act. Sometimes right acts have forbidden parts or aspects. Kant's choice of the agent's maxim as the relevant point for moral assessment recognizes that various aspects and components of any act may be morally important, but Anscombe's suggestion requires us to focus on a single aspect of each act, which may in the first place not be the one that we judge most important for moral assessment.

One further and quite distinct approach to the problem of identifying the

[10] *Ibid.*, p. 39.

act description relevant for moral assessment is made by D'Arcy in *Human Acts*.[11] Like Anscombe, he begins by considering series of descriptions of one act where each member of the series can be regarded as stating a means to the ends stated by its successor (again with the proviso that these means and ends are not necessarily successive). Unlike Anscombe, he does not require that the descriptions in these series be intentional act descriptions. Descriptions such as "contracting the finger muscles" can occur in his series of descriptions of acts. He then points out that in many cases we may elide one term of a series into the term that denotes its consequences. We may redescribe "firing a gun" as "shooting a man" or "singing a song" as "entertaining people" if in each case that was what happened. But certain descriptions are privileged and so may not be elided in this way. "Killing babies" may not be redescribed as "aiding medical research" even if it does so; "A deceived B with the consequence that he won his vote" may not be redescribed as "A won B's vote." "Some elements, or combinations of elements, are such that, whenever they are present, they verify an autonomous act description." [12] The question, of course, is how these elements are to be identified.

D'Arcy's answer is that they are "cases" of morally significant action for which a special vocabulary of "case terms" has been developed. Case terms are those words or concise phrases which apply to recurrent and important events of a particular sort. Medicine uses case terms to name diseases; sports develop them to refer to particular plays and situations such as "lobs" and "smashes." In moral discourse

> even the most originally contrived deeds [can be] subsumed under the traditional case terms, which have been fashioned because of the frequent occurrence of such deeds and the special importance they have for human happiness and welfare.[13]

Examples of moral case terms are "murder," "rape," "adultery," and "theft" (these are "moral species terms") and more general terms such as "dishonesty," "justice," and "unchastity" (these are "moral genus terms").

It is true that we have this vocabulary of case terms in the field of moral as of other sorts of discourse. But if their occurrence in act descriptions is to be the basis for selecting those act descriptions relevant for moral assessment, then we need some criterion other than intuition by which to identify moral case terms. This D'Arcy does not provide. His reference to the "special im-

[11] E. D'Arcy, *Human Acts*.   [12] *Ibid.*, p. 21.   [13] *Ibid.*, p. 24.

portance they have for human happiness and welfare" perhaps points to his actual use of some sort of utilitarian criterion in deciding what is and what is not a moral case term. But this criterion is never explicitly formulated. He speaks of a "special point of view" of moral judgment which cannot prescind from "matters affecting the welfare of ourselves and others." [14] There is no reason to suppose that this particular criterion will select a single description of any act as relevant for moral assessment. In one of D'Arcy's examples a sheriff is seen as organizing a judicial murder to forestall a lynching of several persons. Both these act descriptions bear on human happiness and welfare, though very differently. If neither of these terms is to be elided, is their conjunction to be assessed? If this is so, D'Arcy's criterion for selecting morally relevant act descriptions, when precisely formulated, will turn out to be equivalent to Lyons', which is incompatible with Kant's ethical theory. Even if elision of act descriptions under case terms were compatible with Kant's theory, it would eliminate the possibility of assessing minor aspects and components of acts. D'Arcy's solution to the problem of relevant act descriptions therefore cannot help us in contexts of moral assessment.

None of these methods for selecting an act description has succeeded in selecting the one which is relevant for Kantian assessments of right. For the time being, we can do no more with Kant's theory of right in contexts of assessment than to say whether the agent decided rightly. In cases where his maxim was inappropriate either to his situation or to his act we may also be able to say something about the reasons for this inappropriateness. We might, for instance, classify the reasons for the inappropriateness of his maxim in ways such as those J. L. Austin suggests in "A Plea For Excuses." [15] Did the agent arrive at his inappropriate maxim carelessly or inadvertently; was he mistaken or misled? Did an agent fail to act on his maxim owing to circumstances which he should have foreseen, or can he be excused for botching the job? In some cases we might be able to assess the rightness or wrongness of his act of coming to a decision. But a judgment of the deontic status of the act of deciding on an inappropriate maxim will not automatically yield a judgment of the deontic status of the act done on that maxim.

So if we are to find a way of extending Kant's theory of right to contexts of

[14] *Ibid.,* p. 28.

[15] J. L. Austin, "A Plea for Excuses," in *Philosophical Papers,* ed. J. O. Urmson and G. J. Warnock, pp. 123–52.

assessment, some further solution to the problem of relevant descriptions is still needed. Neither reliance on the agent's maxim nor any of the theories just examined can meet the requirements of an adequate solution to this problem. Any adequate solution must state an effective criterion of selection that is generally applicable and yields plausible results. I cannot offer any solution which meets these standards. But this is a lack which I regard with some detachment. Kant's theory of right can at least be used in contexts of decision and action. And it is these contexts which are of most importance for the moral life. If there were no contexts of decision, there would be no contexts of assessment. The first task of an ethical theory is not to enable us to pass judgment on others.

Even if the Categorical Imperative proves unjustifiable, Kant's solution to the problem of relevant descriptions may be worth retaining. Any nonteleological ethical theory faces the problem of deciding how acts should be described. A Kantian solution to this problem will leave us with contexts of assessment where no theory of right leads to conclusions, but it will not leave us unable to discover what we ought to do.

BIBLIOGRAPHY

❦ *Works by Immanuel Kant*

All references to Kant's works are to the edition of the Prussian Academy of Sciences. References in footnotes use the abbreviations given on the left; quotations are taken from the translations given on the right.

Kant's gesammelte Schriften. 24 vols. Berlin: herausgegeben von der Königlich Preussischen Akademie der Wissenschaften, 1902–66.

G.	*Grundlegung zur Metaphysik der Sitten* (1911), IV, 387–463. Translated by H. J. Paton, as "The Groundwork of the Metaphysics of Morals," in H. J. Paton, *The Moral Law*. Rev. ed. London, Hutchinson, 1953, pp. 53–131.
K.P.V.	*Kritik der Praktishen Vernunft* (1913), V, 1–163. Translated by T. K. Abbott as "Critique of Practical Reason," in T. K. Abbott, *Kant's Critique of Practical Reason and Other Works on the Theory of Ethics.* 6th ed. London: Longmans, 1959, pp. 87–262; L. W. Beck, *Critique of Practical Reason.* New York: Bobbs-Merrill, Library of Liberal Arts, 1956.
M.S.	*Die Metaphysik der Sitten* (1914), VI, 203–491. Part I (the "Rechtslehre") translated by J. Ladd as *The Metaphysical Elements of Justice.* New York, Bobbs-Merrill, Library of Liberal Arts, 1965. Part II (the "Tugendlehre") translated by M. J. Gregor as *The Doctrine of Virtue* (with introduction to the whole work and all of prefaces to Part I). Where a passage occurs both in the Gregor and in the Ladd translation, the Gregor is used. New York, Harper and Row, 1964.
	Über ein vermeintes Recht aus Menschenliebe zu Lügen (1923), VIII, 425–30. Translated by T. K. Abbott as "On a Supposed Right To Tell Lies from Benevolent Motives," in T. K. Abbott, *Kant's Critique of Practical Reason and Other Works on the Theory of Ethics.* 6th ed. London: Longmans, 1959. Appendix I, pp. 361–65.

✳️ *Other Works*

Anscombe, G. E. M. *Intention.* Oxford: Basil Blackwell, 1958.

Austin, J. L. *Philosophical Papers,* ed. J. O. Urmson and G. J. Warnock. Oxford: Clarendon Press, 1961.

Axinn, S. "Kant, Authority and the French Revolution," *Journal of the History of Ideas,* 32 (1971), 423–32.

Baier, K. *The Moral Point of View: A Rational Basis of Ethics.* Ithaca, N.Y.: Cornell University Press, 1958.

Beck, L. W. "Apodictic Imperatives," *Kant-Studien,* 49 (1957), 7–23.

——— *A Commentary on Kant's Critique of Practical Reason.* Chicago: University of Chicago Press, 1960.

——— "Kant and the Right of Revolution," *Journal of the History of Ideas,* 32 (1971), 411–22.

Broad, C. D. *Five Types of Ethical Theory.* Totowa, N.J.: Littlefield Adams, 1965 (reprinted).

Chisholm, R. "Supererogation and Offence," *Ratio,* 5 (1963), 1–14.

D'Arcy, E. *Human Acts: An Essay in Their Moral Evaluation.* Oxford: Clarendon Press, 1963.

Dietrichson, P. "When Is a Maxim Fully Universalizable?" *Kant-Studien,* 55 (1964), 143–70.

Duncan, A. R. C. *Practical Reason and Morality.* Edinburgh: Nelson, 1967.

Ebbinghaus, J. "Interpretation and Misinterpretation of the Categorical Imperative," trans. H. J. Paton, *Philosophical Quarterly,* 4 (1954), 97–108.

Eisenberg, P. "Basic Ethical Categories of Kant's *Tugendlehre,*" *American Philosophical Quarterly,* 3 (1966), 255–69.

Ewing, A. C. "The Paradoxes of Kant's Ethics," *Philosophy,* XIII (1938), 40–56.

Gregor, M. J. *Laws of Freedom. A Study of Kant's Method of Applying the Categorical Imperative in the Metaphysik der Sitten.* Oxford: Basil Blackwell, 1963.

Grice, G. R. *The Grounds of Moral Judgement.* Cambridge: Cambridge University Press, 1967.

Haezrahi, P. "The Concept of Man as End-in-Himself," reprinted in *Kant: A Collection of Critical Essays,* ed. R. P. Wolff. London: Macmillan, 1968.

Hare, R. M. *Freedom and Reason.* Oxford: Clarendon Press, 1963.

Hill, T. E. "Kant on Imperfect Duty and Supererogation," *Kant-Studien,* 62 (1971), 55–76.

Kemp, J. "Kant's Examples of the Categorical Imperative," *Philosophical Quarterly,* 8 (1958), 63–71.

Körner, S. *Kant.* Harmondsworth, Middlesex: Penguin Books Ltd., 1955.

Locke, D. "The Trivializability of Universalizability," *Philosophical Review,* LXXVII (1968), 25–44.

Luce, R. D. and H. Raiffa. *Games and Decisions.* New York: Wiley & Sons Inc., 1957.

Lyons, D. *Forms and Limits of Utilitarianism.* Oxford: Clarendon Press, 1965.

Melden, A.I., ed., *Essays in Moral Philosophy.* Seattle, Wash.: University of Washington Press, 1958.

Mill, J. S. *Utilitarianism* in *Utilitarianism, Liberty and Representative Government.* London: Everyman's Library, J. M. Dent & Sons Ltd., 1968 (reprinted).

Moritz, M. *Kant's Einteilung der Imperative.* Copenhagen: Munksgaard, 1960.

Paton, H. J. *The Moral Law.* Rev. ed., London: Hutchinson & Co. Ltd., 1953.

—— "An Alleged Right to Lie: A Problem in Kantian Ethics," *Kant-Studien,* 45 (1953–54), 190–203.

—— *The Categorical Imperative.* London: Hutchinson & Co. Ltd., 1958.

Prichard, H. A. *Moral Obligation.* Oxford: Clarendon Press, 1949.

Ross, W. D. *The Right and the Good.* Oxford: Clarendon Press, 1930.

—— *Kant's Ethical Theory.* Oxford: Clarendon Press, 1954.

Simon, M. *Models of Man.* New York: Wiley & Sons Inc., 1957.

Singer, M. G. *Generalization in Ethics: An Essay in the Logic of Ethics with the Rudiments of a System of Moral Philosophy.* New York: Alfred A. Knopf, 1961.

Urmson, J. O. "Saints and Heroes," in *Essays in Moral Philosophy,* ed. A. I. Melden. Seattle, Wash.: University of Washington Press, 1958.

Williams, T. C. *The Concept of the Categorical Imperative: A Study of the Place of the Categorical Imperative in Kant's Ethical Theory.* Oxford: Clarendon Press, 1968.

Wolff, R. P. *The Autonomy of Reason: A Commentary on Kant's Groundwork of the Metaphysic of Morals.* New York: Harper & Row, 1973.

INDEX